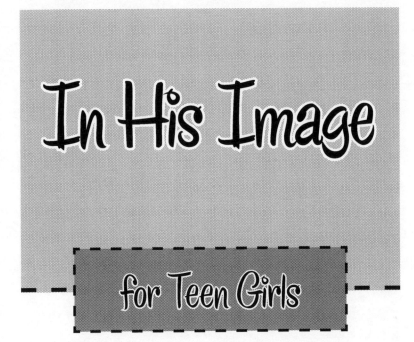

In His Image

for Teen Girls

Priscilla Soos

WESTBOW
PRESS®
A DIVISION OF THOMAS NELSON
& ZONDERVAN

WestBow Press books may be ordered through booksellers or by contacting:

WestBow Press
A Division of Thomas Nelson & Zondervan
1663 Liberty Drive
Bloomington, IN 47403
www.westbowpress.com
1 (866) 928-1240

ISBN: 978-1-5127-0276-7 (sc)
ISBN: 978-1-5127-0275-0 (hc)
ISBN: 978-1-5127-0274-3 (e)

Print information available on the last page.

WestBow Press rev. date: 12/07/2015

Table of Contents

Preface

When my husband and I discovered that we were pregnant for the third time, I decided to have a good old-fashioned sit-down with God; my plan was to place my order. The conversation was very one-sided and went something like this:

"You know God, I already have two boys, all the stuff for two boys, and frankly, it would be easier for me if this one was also a boy." It did not work out like that.

When the doctor, filled with excitement, gave us the news that we were having a girl, my joy did not quite match his. While he chatted about pink nurseries and little dresses, my gut filled with fear. Fear of what? Fear of how I was going to raise a daughter in this world? To make things even more interesting, God filled me with a hypersensitivity to how the world speaks to girls through media—music, television, movies, magazines, and books. God showed me how girls took those messages into their friendships and relationships with boys, how they apply those messages to the way they make decisions, and how those messages shape their self-images.

The fear swept over me. While processing all the information God was giving me I could not think of a way that my voice alone could be louder than all the noise coming from everywhere else. After exhausting myself, I finally cried out to God, "How will I raise a daughter who has confidence in herself, who has a strength balanced in softness, and who is a leader and not a follower?"

I felt God tell me that I would not be doing it alone. I had an ally, a strong and powerful ally. God wanted me to put Him on the front line and follow Him straight through the battlefield. I also felt Him telling me not to be selfish, focusing only on my daughter and wishing the rest of the girls good fortune on their fight. Instead, He wanted me to tell my story—the journey I have taken in my life and my journey with my daughter. The good, the bad, and the ugly.

My prayer is that you will find your own way with this book, through not only my rights and wrongs, but also through God. What I feel God has given me to share is a message that you are created in God's image. There is a new life for girls who follow God. We don't have to be pressed down by this world; we must live the life of God's daughters—a life of value, strength, and focus, knowing who we are in Christ.

1

In His Image

This chapter is meant to provide an understanding of what it means to be created in God's image. Lifetimes are spent trying to answer the question, "Who am I?" In learning this you will bring value, strength, and focus to your life.

In His Image

Then God said, "Let us make man in our image, in our likeness, and let him rule" (Genesis 1:26–27).

For you created my inmost being; you knit me together in my mother's womb. I praise you because I am fearfully and wonderfully made; your works are wonderful (Psalm 139:13–14). The brother in humble circumstances ought to take pride in his high position (James 1:9).

God saw all that he had made, and it was very good (Genesis 1:31).

Why is it so important to know who I am in Christ?

Every day we set out on our lifelong quest to answer the question, "Who am I?" Lifetimes are spent spinning our wheels, going through our ideas of who we are. When we run out of those, we start searching in other places, looking to family, friends, and the media. Once we have completely exhausted ourselves, we will look to God as a last resort. My hope is that by the end of this book you will begin and continue your quest through a life with God first.

What is God's Image?

Our opening verse explains that we are created in the image and likeness of God. So what is God's image? God is many things. One of those things is a king. *"God, the blessed and only Ruler, the King of kings and Lord of lords" (1 Timothy 6:15).* There is also the image of a Father. *"A father to the fatherless" (Psalm 68:5).* When your Father is a king, by birthright you have a claim to nobility.

My husband is in the restaurant business. By birthright my kids have been exposed to this business. From the time they started eating table food, my kids have been experiencing some of the best restaurants in the Twin Cities. While most kids were eating boxed macaroni and cheese my kids were eating lobster macaroni and cheese, prepared by some of the top chefs in the area. When they go to one of the restaurants my husband heads up they are recognized by the staff and treated differently. They are given the best table and the best server. Everyone checks on them to make sure they are satisfied. All of this special treatment is because of who their father is.

There is a privilege that comes to you as a child of God.

What is nobility?

When you look up the word *noble* in Webster's dictionary many definitions apply, but my favorite is number six: "of an admirably high quality." Wow, being a child of God means we are noble or "of admirably high quality!"

Acknowledge your true value.

When Adam and Eve sinned by eating the apple, their eyes opened and they realized they were naked. They sewed fig leaves together and made coverings for themselves; when they heard God in the garden, they hid from Him. God called to them, and Adam replied, "I heard you in the garden, and I was afraid because I was naked, so I hid." I love Gods response: "Who told you that you were naked?" (Genesis 3:7–11).

Once Adam and Eve ate the apple, they had an image of themselves that was no longer that of God but instead one for this world.

At this stage of life, most of what you know about yourself is what others have told you. For example, "My mom says I'm funny," "My teacher says I'm smart," or "People always say I'm pretty."

Science class taught us that two random atoms collided and from that collision we emerged out of the muck and developed into the form we take today. We then use this information to decide how we will view ourselves. The part that is not taught in science class is: you cannot live to your fullest potential on just the information given to you by the world.

Who are you?

God has planted in each of us a seed filled with our gifts, talents, and promises that make us who we are. *"If you belong to Christ, then you are Abraham's seed, and heirs according to the promise"* (Galatians 3:29).

> *For you have been born again, not of perishable seed, but of imperishable seed, through the living and enduring word of God. For all men are like grass, and all their glory is like the flowers of the field; the grass withers and the flowers fall, but the word of the Lord stands forever. And this is the word that was preached to you. (1 Peter 1:23–25).*

What is meant by a seed planted inside of me?

What is a seed? Seems like a silly question. When looking at a seed, it's nothing fancy. Usually a bean-looking thing, with no exciting coloring and small in size, but that seed is the beginning.

A rose starts as a seed. You plant your seed in good soil, you nurture it, and in time the beginnings of a rose will push through the icky, dense dirt and blossom into a beautiful flower. But it all starts with that seed.

Another good example is a caterpillar. When a caterpillar is born, that caterpillar has the makings of a butterfly inside itself.

Right now you are in seed form. You are in caterpillar form. A rose starts under the dirt but ends in glory under the sun. A caterpillar is a worm crawling on its belly until its time of glory when it turns into a butterfly and flies away. How does the seed know to grow or the caterpillar to transform? The information is already in them. All that seed does is accept what it is and grow. The rose never tries to be a caterpillar, and the caterpillar never tries to be a rose.

What is God's plan for me?

After each one of God's creations, He made the statement, *"It is good" (Genesis 1:31)*. Actually in my NIV bible it says "VERY GOOD" Why would God say that? He said that because the things that He made were the way He intended them to be, and He was pleased with them as they were. This includes you and me.

Value and focus are created when you know who you are.

Those who do not amount to much, by this world's standards, should rejoice in their position as those whom God loves.

Throughout your life people will use you based on what they need from you.

It is not always something done intentionally; it's that we are unable to lift others higher than we are in our lives.

How much are you putting into sending out the right image of yourself? What is your image saying about you right now? When you walk into a room, how do people see you? Your image follows you everywhere. Your image tells people how to treat you. When I was eighteen my mom moved from the inner city to the suburbs. I remember when my Black intercity friends and I used to go into those suburban stores. I noticed that security followed us every time. We used to make a game of it and split up in different directions and make them chase us throughout the store. Most people would find this racist on the part of security. Maybe, but it is more likely they followed us because we made easy targets. We were the only black kids in the store, and we were running around like crazy people. We could have chosen a different behavior that made us of no interest to them. Instead the way we acted created an image of suspicion not only for us, but for the next group of black kids that came into that store as well.

The first step to change is knowing you need to change.

Start to make the decision in your life to change and examine who you are. It sounds so simple, but in fact this can be one of the most difficult things to do. It is easy for us to judge a stranger, or tell a family member or friends what they need to do. Very few have the courage to look inside themselves and be who God created them to be. It is easier to become another face in the crowd.

Many of us create our images based on what voices are the loudest in our lives. Mom is pressuring me to be a cheerleader because she was a cheerleader, and my sister was a cheerleader. Media says it is up to them to tell you who you are, what you will wear and what trends you will follow. TV says to be popular you just need to copy the characters in their movies or shows. Rap music rarely speaks positively about women. Under all of that, down in your core, is a whisper from God trying to lead you to your true self. How do you do it; how do you change? Start at the beginning.

You will face difficulty when you start to make changes.

Is change difficult? Oh yeah. Change is a really difficult because we are creatures of comfort. We like things easy and fast. Change is neither easy or fast, and for sure uncomfortable. When someone starts to make improvements for him or herself, even if the change is small, there will be opposition from both the people around you, as well as yourself.

Remembering where you came from is very different from staying where you are.

Why is it important to remember where you came from? I heard a preacher say once "the tests in your life are your testimony." Which means the experiences in your life are learning opportunities. Some are there to make sure that you don't go backwards in your life. Some are there to light your path. Some are there to show others the way.

Remembering where you came from does not mean you have to stay where you are. Did you know that daughters of teen mothers are more likely to become teen mothers themselves? Statistics also say that children from poor families are less likely to succeed in the classroom or life. They (whoever they are) say that poor families produce future poor families. These are images that others put on us, and we fully accept. We also do this to each other. Cheerleaders date football players. The A students are uncool geeks and nerds. If you come from a certain neighborhood then you are less acceptable than others.

I live on the north side of Minneapolis. This summer the news called my neighborhood "Murder-apolis". My kids go to school in the affluent Wayzata school district. When the kids of this suburban school hear where my kids are from, they often ask - "Have you seen any drive-by shootings?" "Have you been robbed?" "Are there drug dealers everywhere?" The questions go on and on. But they all stem from the image of where we live.

If you come from a place that is not where you want to be, remembering is your motivation to move forward. God created us to move forward. We only have faces in the front. Our eyes can only see forward. Our mouth pushes sound forward, and our ears are shaped to hear forward, thus the term "talking behind your back". Our arms bend to reach and grab forward. How hard is it to scratch that itch you get in the middle of your back? Legs are designed to move you forward. That's why you get off balance when you try to run backwards. You are not designed to go back. The only thing designed in the back is the butt, to sit and produce waste behind you. So remember where you came from but focus on where you are going.

Your environment can make an image change seem impossible

You may be in a place that is constantly telling you that you are not good enough, or you will never be more than what you are right now. It seems like unreasonable goals are placed on you. There may be pressure to be an overachiever or to be the best at a sport. Maybe Mom is trying to relive her childhood as the star cheerleader or basketball player. Or pushing you to fill a heavy class schedule to gain a college's attention.

I was speaking with some parents at my daughter's school about a birthday party we were being invited to (she's ten). One of the mothers explained that her daughter was unable to attend the party because her daughter is in basketball and soccer, and Mom pushes her to be the best in the classroom. She goes on to explain that this is because she wants her daughter to earn a scholarship for college (again, she's ten). I thought about it for a minute as she proudly recounted their seven-day-a-week packed schedule. I realized that we were eight years from graduation day and thought about all the money this mom was spending on private lessons, team travel, gas, eating out, team fees, and so on. She could invest that money in a college fund, giving her daughter a guarantee on college money, not just a hope for a scholarship. Her daughter was missing so many things because of her overwhelming schedule: birthday parties, after school events, and just time to hang out. When Mia and her friends got together, nine out of ten invites for this girl were met with scheduling conflicts.

How do I change directions when it seems like there is so much wrong?

"I tell you the truth, if you have faith as small as a mustard seed, you can say to this mountain, Move from here to there and it will move. Nothing will be impossible for you" (Matthew 17:20-21). Those mountains could be a bad attitude, a bad relationship,

wrong choices, etc. A new beginning in the family of Christ levels the playing field. Where you came from no longer has power over you. Who your parents are, how much money you have, or past bad decisions. None of these things have power over you any longer.

"Follow my example as I follow the example of Christ." (*1 Corinthians 11:1*) or in other words, fake it till you make it. Cognitive dissonance: an official term that means if you behave a certain way, your beliefs will eventually change to conform to your behavior. Or to put it plainly, fake it till you make it. You must find your own way at some point, because you cannot imitate others forever. But until then, fake it till you make it.

"A student is not above his teacher but a perfectly trained student is like his teacher" (Luke 6:40). This is a good point. You must be mindful of who your teachers are, remembering that you will become like your teacher. This is not always a school teacher. You may not even realize you are being taught. I had a friend in the sixth grade who thought me how to smoke a cigarette. I also had a friend who taught me the proper way to apply makeup so I did not look like a clown.

Where am I going with this? We imitate others every day. When we were little girls we tried on Mom's shoes, snuck into her makeup, piled on all her jewelry. We copied Mom when we played with our dolls. We got into an older sister's closet. As we get older, we copy friends. Movie stars. We copy the way they speak, dress, hair styles. We let magazines tell us the latest fashions and trends we must follow. But the best example given tends to go uncopied, and that is Jesus. He lived a life for us to emulate.

You (strong on the "you"), have to take things into your own hands.

Challenge yourself in areas where you need growth, areas you will see as accomplishments. Seeing growth is a reward that keeps you focused. Each time you have an accomplishment, it will lift you a little higher.

I was not a good reader. I hated reading out loud (and still do). If we had to read around the room in class, I would count out the lines to see where it would land on me, and practice my line before my turn. (I still do this today.) When I was younger, instead of practicing reading, I avoided it. I only focused on the subjects I enjoyed, such as my speech and writing classes. During that time I did not know how to shut off slang and speak properly in a professional environment, and my writing skills also suffered. Well, guess what: reading helps you improve both writing and speaking skills. Go figure.

I took it upon myself to read to increase my vocabulary. When I first started reading, I treated it like a homework assignment. I assigned myself one chapter a day. The first book I read was *Red Dragon* (the prequel to *The Silence of the Lambs*); I had nightmares but I finished. Over time I began to love reading. Once I got into it, I added personal growth books to my library. Everything you want to know, someone has written a book on it. On the same note, when I am at home talking with friends, I can get right back into the slang. You do not have to give up trends, but you do need to know how to put yourself in check.

If you are struggling in class, get help from your teachers, or ask the "smart kid" in class. You will see accomplishments with the increases in your grades. I was a C student, mainly because a C was all the effort I put into school. This is a huge deal. I hope none of my high school teachers are reading this. I am a very clever person. It is one of my gifts. When I was younger, I used that gift for evil. I invented books for book reports: the story lines, authors, the whole bit. I once won a writing contest in the seventh grade that was supposed to be a family research paper. I skipped all the research and made up a grandfather and his entire life. My story was printed in the newspaper (you can imagine my mom's reaction, it was not pleasant). Luckily, my grandfather never saw it. Sadly, the list of homework scams went on and on.

My choices in school never leaned on the side of homework. School was a social outlet, and homework interfered with that. When I graduated high school and went to college, reality quickly sunk in. I was not prepared. I was floored by how little I actually knew. I am still facing those poor decisions today on the job. I have to spend time relearning things I should have learned when I was in school.

Another part to making changes is controlling your schedule: if college is your goal, make sure you are in tune with the school's requirements. If you are uninformed you may be overdoing it for no benefit. Also learn the word "No". If your focus is college prep do not get talked into working on the pep rally.

I allowed my friend to talk me into joining the track team, which was really funny because I hated track. Also, I sucked at it. I lost every race I ran, most of the time in last place. There was a motive to joining track. During the off season, coaches would have their teams join track to stay active. The track team was filled with football, basketball, and baseball players. Can you see where my focus was? I can tell you where it was not. It was not in the practices. It was not in the all day long track meets and the sheer humiliation of losing week after week. It also was not in dance line, which I truly enjoyed but walked away from. I even ended up dating a guy that was not on the track team. To this day I hate running and would only consider it if I were being chased, and even then I would evaluate the scale of the threat first. Ugh, such wasted time.

A big part of our image is our peer group and the choices we make.

Picture a red balloon on a string. That balloon cannot rise any higher than that string which is tied around your wrist. That string is used to pull the balloon down when needed to go under a tree or get in a car and released again to float, but only to the length of that string. Though if untied it has enough helium to float up to the clouds.

If you find yourself in a group that is no longer going in the direction you want to go, you have to pull up the courage from within and change your direction. Get yourself into something that takes up your time, like a sports team, a club, a band, or a job. When your friends challenge the new way you are spending your time, have your story prepared. I have practice (with the new group you joined). My mom is on my back. If I don't get my act together I'll be grounded or lose my car, etc.

You may find that school has nothing to offer but a great education and that's fine. Use school for what it was intended, to learn. I know we all watch those high school movies and even reality shows about how great our experience at school should be, but you may need to get your friends elsewhere. Like the Boys and Girls Club, a sports club, a singing group.

Make friends with the kids from the neighborhood who do not go to your school, in church groups, family, get an after school job, etc.

Changing direction requires one step at a time.

Trying to change everything at once is overwhelming. This may leave you feeling defeated. Start small and move up. This is the time that you have to honestly look at, what you have and what you want. Then start to make the changes needed to get there.

What attention are the boys paying you? Are they gone quickly after they get what they want? The change in direction is to stop giving them what they want. This is an affection and esteem issue. You need to find that from within you. I missed three days of school this week; the change in direction is to make a commitment to go every day next week. I did not complete any homework assignments; the change in direction is to start to complete homework. Doing the assigned work for the day and one past due assignment. My friends are a distraction; the change of direction here is to hang out less. Set a curfew for yourself, that you must be home by nine.

Fill your Head

Your mind has to be stimulated or it will stimulate itself by tricking you. You can find yourself feeling happy or content in a bad situation or relationship. There is an adrenalin rush from being in a fight, or doing something wrong and not getting caught. The hormonal rush from sex. These are all false feelings of good. And if that is all you are feeding your mind, your mind can get so full of false emotions that you can no longer tell the difference between the real good and the false good.

If your life is filled with negative friends, negative boyfriends, a negative home life, a negative school experience, you are placing a negative attitude on yourself. Your mind is dominated by negativity. Your mind will piece together what it finds as joy in that negative. Food, sex, drugs, achievements. Your mind can go as far as to squeeze out any genuine good that tries to leak in.

So how do you retrain your brain to recognize genuine good?

My favorite is journaling. It gives you a physical reference. Take notes on the situations that you are facing, how you responded in that situation, and the outcome. Such as *I had a test in math class today, but I gave in when my friends pressured me to skip. Now I will only get partial credit for a make up test. Keeping my grade at a D.* Why did you give in? Were you fearful of missing out? Journal also what you did. *We hid out in some park because we did not want to be spotted by the cops. It was a boring afternoon.*

Seeing your choice (to skip the test), why you did it (I didn't want to miss out), and the outcome (I will only get partial credit on my test) and (it wasn't worth it, I would not have been missing anything). This gives you a real way of seeing the truths, and next time you will know it is not worth it.

Making changes is never easy and it can be even harder when you are young. Youth is a time when all you want is to fit in. That is understandable, but you have to make a decision about what you are trying to fit into. "Goals" is a word thrown at you right and left. How do you make goals? What is a goal? Making goals is making a commitment and that commitment gives you focus.

You should have different goals. Small goals could be to clean your room or finish your homework. Call your grandma for her birthday. A medium goal could be to try something new today, make the debate team. Or a large goal of getting into college, remaining a virgin, or resisting the pressure to do drugs. Each goal will have sub-goals; for example, to get my room clean, I need to miss the movie tonight. To make the debate team, I need to practice after basketball practice although I am tired. To stay a virgin, I need to turn away from the intense pressure from my friends, media, and must be up front with my boyfriend.

Goals should be written down in a journal. Posted on the bathroom mirror. So when they are accomplished you can see what you have done. Or the flip side if they are not accomplished you are reminded to refocus. Goals and commitments give you focus. They give you direction. Make goals and stick to them.

This is your life you must choose. (Deuteronomy 30:19-20) You can change no matter what, you just have to change your focus.

3

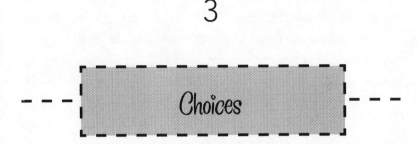

Choices

aking choices in your life is something you cannot escape. Every day you are forced to make one decision after the next. Refusing to make a choice is even making a choice. The idea of it can be overwhelming, but if you spend your life reacting to your situations you will struggle to have any growth in your life.

> I have set before you life and death, blessing and curses. Now choose life that you may love the Lord your God, listen to his voice, and hold fast to him. (Deuteronomy 30:19-20)

Everyone has a will, the freedom to make choices in their own lives. Change requires that the right choices be made for the needed change. This takes practice. The fantasy of waving a magic wand and instantly changing our situations keeps us stuck.

It can be hard to understand when you are in the moment. It may even seem like you are getting away with bad choices, but you're not. *"For the word of God is living and active. Sharper than any doubled edge sword, it penetrates even to dividing soul and spirit, joints and marrow; it judges the thought and attitudes of the heart. Nothing in all creation is hidden from God's sight. Everything is uncovered and laid bare before the eyes of him to whom we must give account "(Hebrews 4:12-13).*

The consequences may not be the ones expected or obvious, like punishment from a parent, suspension from school, or pregnancy. Instead you miss out on the blessings your life should have. You will have a feeling that something is missing in your life. You will find more unhappiness, conflict, and struggles. Things will not be easy. You will find betrayal, hurt, and a lack of growth or movement in your life.

If you throw a white feather into the wind, that feather is instantly at the wind's mercy. That feather has no choice but to go in whatever direction the wind carries it. The wind will have no concern for the feather's beauty. The wind will drag it through the mud with no regard for how delicate the feather is. The wind will smash it into things until the wind has died away or the feather is so damaged it can no longer fly. That once beautiful feather will be dropped to the ground and left behind.

Making choices will give you weight so that you are no longer light as a feather but instead solid as a rock. You can get so solid you will be able to catch other feathers that blow into you.

The dark side of choice is the fear of making one.

A good way to get through the fear of making new choices is to journal. Journal the situation you are in and the choices you made to get through it. Then you have a reference to look back on, which will help you get through to the next set of choices.

-I want to join the debate team and none of my friends are on the team.

-Journal your fears about joining:

1. I'm afraid I won't be good at debate.
2. I'm afraid my friends won't approve.
3. I'm afraid my boyfriend will be upset that it takes more of our time away.

-Then journal the reality:

1. They gave me a lot of training so at first I wasn't any good, but I am getting better. Next year I will be able to start.
2. My friends had no issue at all with my joining, they barely noticed
3. My boyfriend gave me a lot of attitude at first, but backed off when he realized I wasn't quitting.

You will notice that your fears can outweigh reality more often than not. And when the worst does happen, it is not as traumatic as you feared.

Be strong. Making choices is scary. Choices can put you in some tough spots, but with each one you make, the process will get easier. Not just for you to make but for others to accept. Once you become a solid decision maker, those around you will realize that you will not be swayed and they will accept you and your choices.

Your Spiritual Conscience

God fills us with his Spirit. This spirit is our earthly guide, our comforter, and our conscience, among other things.

What is a conscience?

It is the pinch or uneasy feeling you get in your gut or the thought in your head telling you to think twice, to reconsider, to go the other way. The feeling you have of regret or shame when you have overridden it. Each time you push through your conscience, that pinch will get softer and softer until you have completely numbed it. The spirit of God will never leave you, but once you turn away from Him negative feelings such as anger, fear, and depression will show up. The unspiritual side of your conscience is a very dark place.

Knowing yourself means taking a truthful look at you.

When you are bothered by something someone else is doing, God may be showing you that this is something in you. I talk a lot. I like to control every conversation I am in. The first time someone I am in a conversation with pauses to take a breath, I am quick to steal the conversation back. I have the nerve to be irritated by others who talk too much. I recognize that this is something I do, so I have to be very conscious in a group conversation. Sometimes I have to say to myself "time to stop talking and allow others to have their time."

Change requires focus. God gave you a great gift in the Holy Spirit to help in your decision making, but you have to pay attention to it.

How do you change a bad attitude?

Bad attitudes are reflections of your inner self. You are playing out what is going on inside you. Pride is a big driver of a bad attitude. You have to have the last word, period. It is your way or no way. Anyone who comes against you is the enemy.

Your bad attitude is no different than those two-year-olds rolling around on the floor screaming and crying. You may not display the screaming and crying but the emotions are the same. The reason that two-year-old is having the fit is:

1. They lack proper communication skills and do not know how to properly express their feelings.

2. A two-year-old has "the world revolves around me" and "I am its center" view on life.

3. They are frustrated and do not know how to get the results they are looking for without the fit.

4. They don't understand why they cannot have it their way all the time.

These are the same triggers for a bad attitude that are inside you as you get older: you do not know how to communicate your feelings. You must be the center of everything. You get frustrated and do not know how to change to get a different result.

Are you the one who always has something to say? Is your snappy backtalk to your parents when they say the slightest thing to you causing lots of grief at home? This was a biggie for me. My mom would upset me, and I would pop off, storm to my room and slam the door open and then slam it shut. I slammed the door open so hard once that I put the door knob straight through the wall.

I had quite the flair for the dramatic. The popping off had no value and eventually it became just noise. My mom was not moved by my fit. My mom was glad when I stormed off because she did not want to hear my noise anyway.

I was doing myself no favors with these fits. No one was listening and if I had a valid point it was completely lost in the drama. You have to step away. Take a time out. I had to go to my room (without slamming the door). Sometimes you need to yell into a pillow, walk on the treadmill, or do twenty jumping jacks. It may sound crazy but it works. Once your attitude is in check, you can address the issue that upset you in the first place.

Say something nice even when you do not feel like it. Just as important, do not say anything at all. If you are a person with a bad attitude, choking down words can sometimes feel physically painful. Believe me, I know. The words would fly out of my mouth so fast they were gone before I realized I had spoken. Saying something nice in a situation when I was irritated was next to impossible. Even today, telling my husband I love you and appreciate that you took the trash out, when in my mind I was saying he does not thank me for all I do. Big deal, he took the trash out but I cleaned the whole house, took care of the kids, and did the laundry; who cares about the stupid trash. BUT the peace it brings to the house afterwards is undeniable.

A bad attitude pushes people away. They will never get close to you because of a fear of how you are going to act minute by minute. When you are young you may see your bad attitude as being tough. No one is going to tell me what to do. The fear and pride that is behind that shows through the tough exterior.

The Holy Spirit still speaks to me about this regularly, saying "just shut it." Since I have been working and growing with my attitude, I have less frustration and anger in my life, and I am a better wife, friend, mother, sister, daughter, and representative for God. No one wants to be around the know-it-all who always has to have their way.

Attitude choices are difficult to manage, but they are choices. Some people say "I can't help how I feel," but you can. Once you start to pay attention, the choices will get easier. If I can swallow my words and shut up I promise you anyone can.

Attitude barely scratches the surface on the choices you will make daily. They start right off the bat. Hit snooze for the fourth time or get up... what to wear... will I be an A student today or a D student... will I hang with friends all night or just for a little while and get my homework done... will I do the dishes Mom asked me to do or deal with the consequences... will I stay up late and finish this movie or go to sleep so I can get up in the morning before the third snooze alarm...Choices are everywhere and we will never get them all right, but we can make better ones.

The strongest word in choice making is "no." You will never make improvements if you do not know the power in saying and meaning no. Saying "No" frees you from the wind that smashes you around like a feather. And it is not just saying no to others but also saying no to yourself.

I remember having my eye on a guy and wanting to call him for the tenth time without a single call back from him. I needed to physically sit on the phone to keep myself from calling him. Right now my husband and I are in a challenge to lose ten pounds. As badly as I want to win, I want to eat brownies just as badly.

My kids are not in this challenge and are free to eat sweets. It would be easier if I kept sweets out of the house all together. But if I do not teach myself to say no to the sugar cravings, I will gain the ten pounds back after the challenge. If I had called that boy for the tenth time, it would have been sending him a desperate message that I did not intend.

When you decide to take charge of your life, those first choices will not move the earth beneath you. You may find that the first round of choices are not significant at all. The first choices available to you may only be between a really bad choice, a bad choice, or a slightly bad choice. They all seem bad. So you select "slightly bad." Then the next set of choices will be bad, slightly bad, not so bad. The next set of choices will be, not so bad, okay, good. With each new decision you make, your choices will improve.

If you have dug yourself into a hole, know that you can fill that hole one shovel full at a time. The first shovel will look like no progress has been made. Just keep shoveling and you will fill that hole. I love this story:

The Farmer's Donkey

One day a farmer's donkey fell down into a well. The animal cried piteously for hours as the farmer tried to figure out a way to get him out. Finally he decided it was probably impossible and the animal was old and the well was dry anyway, so it just wasn't worth it to try and retrieve the donkey. So the farmer asked his neighbors to come over and help him cover up the well. they all grabbed shovels and began to shovel dirt into the well.

At first, when the donkey realized what was happening he cried horribly. Then, to everyone's amazement, he quieted down and let out some happy brays. A few shovel loads later, the farmer looked down the well to see what was happening and was astonished at what he saw. With every shovel of dirt that hit his back, the donkey was shaking it off and taking a step up (shifting).

As the farmer's neighbors continued to shovel dirt on top of the animal, he continued to shake it off and take a step up. Pretty soon, to everyone's amazement, the donkey stepped up over the edge of the well and trotted off! (Author unknown)

Choices go beyond saying no to sex, not doing drugs, or turning away from peer pressure. Strengthening and disciplining yourself in the smaller choices will provide a foundation when you are facing the bigger ones. So when you feel the weight of the dirt hit your back, shake it off, pack it under your feet, and take one step closer to the top of your well.

4

Family–Earthly and Spiritual

How do I make the changes needed in my life when I am shadowed by my family and the circumstances of my family that I cannot escape?

There are multiple family structures, but I would like to focus on just a few that I have experienced. I fall into that "Church/Divorced" family: I was raised in a church-going family; missing church was unacceptable. We were one of the first families in and one of the last out. My parents were active in the church, and we were always surrounded by other church families. We could not escape it.

This type of family can be very challenging for a young person. There are very strong expectations of what type of kid you should be. The stereotype from the world of the church's kids is that we are all wild and rebellious. You can grow up feeling like you are in a fishbowl. If you mess up, it can be made public and may turn up as a topic at the church. On the bright side, you do think twice before doing things that are too rebellious. Not only from fear of your parents but fear of what could be said at church next Sunday.

You are expected to be well-behaved. You are expected to be God-filled, You are expected to be a leader. If there were shortages you had to read the scripture, or sing in the choir, or usher. You would not only do it but do it happily. We participated in every church activity. Church was crammed down my throat.

With my first taste of freedom, I fulfilled the stereotype and became very rebellious. That freedom came with my parents' divorce when I was in the eighth grade. My sister, brother, and I lived with my mom while my dad got the church in the divorce. It was an ugly split, which gave me my opening.

My parents' divorce was not the traumatic time for me that everyone wanted it to be. I was expected to act out, blame myself, and be depressed. Because I was not. I was accused of hiding my feelings. One day I realized it could be in my favor to use their divorce against them. I would not do homework. I would skip classes. When I was challenged by teachers, I quickly put on my "poor me" act. I was the victim of my horrible parents' divorce. I would break into tears at school so my friends would fall all over me to lift me up. This act is a book in itself.

I rebelled against the expectations of the church family and manipulated the things around me, using the circumstances of my real family. When all else failed, I blamed it on the divorce. I nearly did not graduate because

I skipped so many classes, and when I was there I did just enough to get by.

My dad needed a life change and decided to become a teacher, and guess what high school he chose to teach in? Yep. Mine. My senior year. No matter, I was so disrespectful I continued doing things my way. I lived with my mother and I knew my parents were so angry with each other that he would never speak to her to tell on me. If he did, I would find some twisted way to make it his fault to my mom, and let him blame her for not controlling me. I was good.

The second family is the "Good" family: I consider this family as the one where people looking in from the outside would see two active and attentive parents working hard for the family, doing what they think is best. This family structure is what everyone dreams up. In these "good" families there are kids going through all the same feelings as everyone else. Yet people do not give them full value because they do not understand. "What do you have to be depressed about?" "Your family has money, your parents are happily married, you have a great home, your mom is your best friend." What problems could they have? There is a misconception that having everything is good. It may mean that parents have long work schedules and miss out on many things you are doing or come home too tired to be involved. Some parents rack up debt to get their kids everything they did not have as kids. These kids can be overlooked and misunderstood as spoiled or whiney, but they just want to be heard.

The final family structure I would like to discuss is the "hard" family. This is a family that just does not seem to make it, financially or emotionally, and has no structure.

The heads of this family may be a parent, a grandparent, or no parent at all. The adult is inattentive to needs, from basic care such as food or household cleanliness to a lack of safety. There may be emotional or physical abuse, drugs or alcohol abuse. The list can go on and on.

I had a friend whose mom died when she was young, and she had to live with an aunt who treated her like a burden. Her aunt's biological children lived a very different life than she did. I remember how sad she was. She would discuss with me how there was no affection or support for her. Her aunt received a check every month for having her in the house and was just waiting for her to get of age when the checks stopped so she could leave. Her aunt reminded her of this repeatedly the closer she would get to eighteen. A modern day Cinderella.

She did everything her cousin did. She was a cheerleader like her cousin and a good student like her cousin. It never changed her aunt's treatment. I remember going to my mom for help because my friend thought if she killed herself she would no longer be a burden to her aunt and could be with her mom. All she wanted was someone to love her.

What should you get from your family?

We all understand that we cannot pick our family. Some of you will come from a textbook family. Others will be from far worse circumstances. You may think no one would understand. Problems at home can span from not being heard to tragic abuse. So what can you do? First, you must understand the purpose of the family, love, safety, values, economics, structure, basic needs, guidance for life, and how to act socially. Where do you get the things that you are not getting at home?

Love. What is the love of God? If you do not feel love at home it is important for you to understand the love of God. There are 324 scripture references to love in my NIV bible. I encourage you to go to the reference guide in the back of your bible and look some of these up. It is not that I do not want to do the work; if you take the time to read these scriptures you will physically feel His love.

Understanding how to trust the love of a God you cannot see or has no physical form to tuck you in at night is difficult for us all. You will see the love of God in the way you need it. It can be in the strength to get through a situation. You can feel Him as warmth in a cold place. You can feel Him as a calm in the middle of a bunch of craziness. You can feel Him as a friend when you are alone. You can see Him as a stranger who lends a helping hand in your time of need, the teacher who shows concern over your behavior, and a light in your dark places.

I had an ugly breakup with a boyfriend. He was my "first love." I was devastated. My mind started to tell me that I could get back at him by hurting myself. I was home alone and curled up in my room on the floor crying and thinking what I could do. I went to the kitchen, got a knife, went back to my room and sat down on the floor holding that knife. We had a little black poodle named Sheba. She came into the room and sat right in my lap. I pushed her away, but she came right back, she was not leaving.

I remember looking into her eyes and she looked sad. Right there I saw God. He will use what it is you need, when you need it. He has spoken through a burning bush, even using a donkey to speak to Balaam in Numbers 22:28. After I recognized what was happening, I was flooded with the thoughts that this boy has already got another girlfriend, actually more than one (thus the break up). He will live a full life, so how would my plan get back at him? I have had other break-ups in my life, but I have never gone to that place again. That is the love of God.

Step one: Journaling is a very helpful way of truthfully recognizing what you are, and are not, getting from your family. You may be in a very strict home and misinterpret that strictness for mistrust, or your parents not hearing you. When actually your parents may have been there and done that, and they are trying to keep you from falling into the same pits of young life. *Only be careful, and watch yourselves closely so that you do not forget the things your eyes have seen or let them slip from your heart as long as you live Teach them to your children (Deuteronomy 4:9).*

My daughter asked me to help her with a writing project. Of course she would. After all, I am a writer. I argued her ideas and tried to lead her in the direction I wanted the story to go. I would have been happier if she would have let me do it all and put her name on it. There was nothing wrong with the story she was writing. It was just not the story I wanted to write. I made that girl so miserable I am thankful she still wants to write. She just asks her dad to help now. This is a classic case of good intentions gone bad. If my daughter did not have a strong personality, I could have discouraged her to the point of quitting altogether.

You need to determine if the discomfort you feel in your family is truth or just an obstacle keeping you from getting your own way. Are your parents mean-spirited or are they putting your best interest first, and you don't like it?

There was a guy in high school that I envied so much because his mom let him do whatever he wanted. He could smoke, he could drink (she would buy it for him as long as he drank at home). He could have friends to his house to drink. He could have girls spend the night at his house. He could even stay out all night and not check in. This made me think how unfair my mom was. At the time this was so cool to me. He smoked weed. He had a car. A life of total freedom. I ran into him about fifteen years later, it was sad because he never found any structure in his life. He was overcoming addition, divorced, and separated from his kids. He was still living with his mother in his late thirties because he was unemployed. That ideal mom that I envied, when compared to my own mom, actually was not as good as she looked.

Step two: Find responsible ways to get what you need. Selling drugs to get Nikes is not responsible. Babysitting, raking leaves, shoveling snow, or getting a job are all responsible choices.

Step three: Forgive. God gave each of us free will. Unfortunately, we make the wrong choices in our lives, which can hurt those around us. You must understand that you are never responsible for the adults around you. Remember that your parents have a past life and you are not responsible for that.

I had my son three years into college, and I never went back to finish. For many years people would ask me where I graduated from college. My standard response was "I did not graduate because I had my son Ryan right after I finished my third year". One day someone asked me this question, and as I delivered my standard response, the Holy Spirit welled up inside me and said "Stop telling that lie, Ryan is not responsible for you not finishing school. You could have gone back one hundred times over by now. You chose not to finish."

It was easier for me to blame Ryan than to admit that I chose not to go back so close to finishing. We make mistakes as parents, but underneath it all, it is a dissatisfaction we have with ourselves that we wrongly put on our kids. It is not right but it happens. Letting my son feel responsible for my "failure" was mean-spirited and unfair.

How can the words on the page be applied to my life?

The Bible shows many examples of things you should be getting at home, and a list of things to look for you may not even realize you are missing:

> Discipline Proverbs 13:1, 15:5, 19:13
>
> Knowledge Deuteronomy 11:18-19
>
> The parents should be the pride of the child
>
> Of noble character Proverbs 31
>
> Children should be provided for 2 Corinthians 12:14 (responsibility does not mean going into debt to get a designer handbag)
>
> Inheritance – Parable of the lost son Luke 15:11-31

CORRECTION

"Discipline your son, and he will give you peace; he will bring delight to your soul". (Proverbs 29:17). Correction is needed in your life or you will not grow. Correction should be directed at the area where it is needed (your attitude is not right today) and should never be insulting (1 Timothy 3:4). There is a clear difference between good correction and what we like to call "tuff love".

You can tell the difference between true correction and someone being hurtful by how it feels. Genuine correction should feel like ripping a bandage off: a swift sting that emotionally hurts a little but is in truth and love. Wrong correction is insulting, strays away from the true issue, and hurts deeply. These actions must be recognized as such and removed from your spirit. *Father, do not exasperate your children; instead bring them up in the training and instruction of The Lord (Ephesians 6:4).*

How do you remove it? There are parents who are not satisfied with themselves and they see themselves in their children. Unfairly and sometimes unconsciously they can attack that part that resembles them or makes them look at themselves. If I feel like a financial failure, and my kids ask me for something I cannot afford, I may lash out at them instead of being honest about our situation. "You're always begging. Every time we come in here you beg, beg, beg. Go sit in the car!"

Your parents could be bitterly divorced, and you may look just like your father. Your mother may be harsh to you because you remind her of him. Maybe you have a behavior like your mother, and your father is harsh to you and spends your time together nit-picking those parts in you that remind him of her.

This is very hard on kids, but you must try to understand that this is not your burden to carry. You are not responsible for the family's financial state. Now throwing a fit because your parent says no is your issue. You are not responsible for the troubles in your parents' relationship. When my parents divorced, it was ugly but it was not my burden to carry.

It hurts to receive negativity. Even as an adult, it is hard not to take on other people's issues, but please see it for what it is -- THEIRS. *"Fathers do not embitter your children or they will become discouraged"* (Colossians 3:21).

Are you causing strife in your home?

When you butt heads with your mom, journal honestly about the tiffs. When you calm down, look over them and see if your mom is truly a nag or should you have shut your sassy mouth and picked up your dinner dishes. What role do you play in your family? Are you like me, turning your parents against each other? Are you trying to parent your parents? Do you know you have the freedom to do whatever you want?

My husband loves to have the family around him after work. He misses out on all the day to day stuff and wants some time after work to catch up. Sometimes when he works late on a school night he will try to encourage the kids to stay up late and watch TV with him. After accepting this offer a few times too many, the kids learned that they are the ones who suffer at school the next morning. Now they are quick to say "I have to go to bed." Sometimes you have to set your own boundaries. My husband is not trying to be hurtful, he misses them and wants to spend time with them. Having the freedom to do what you want does not mean that you have to use it.

Love

My dad is not the warm and fuzzy type. You will not get hugs and kisses from him. In thirty-nine years, I never heard him say "I love you." But I have learned that my dad shows love in many other ways. I had to recognize them for myself. He showed up to every event. Whenever I am in need, he is the first person I call, and I have never been rejected. He shows his love for me with his attention and time. I could be resentful that he never spoke the words, but I would have missed all the other forms of love I did receive.

A family should also teach you social skills (how to act outside of the home).

When our family goes to a fine restaurant, my kids are always complimented on how well they behave. My husband and I taught them how to act. They know how to order, what silverware to use, and have good table manners. Your family may not be into going to fine dining restaurants but having the skills to sit at a table and get through a meal has proven very valuable to me as an adult.

We can treat our families and our ways of doing things as "THE WAY." I had a white friend in college who by mistake said a racial slur about someone else in my face. When I challenged him on it, he first wanted to explain to me that this was the language he heard at home. I was able to keep myself together and we had extensive conversation on the topic. He realized that night how wrong his family was. You have to keep in mind that there is a big world outside of the walls of your home, and just because your mom makes peach cobbler and your friends mom makes peach pie, it does not mean it is wrong, just different.

You may not get the right messages from your family like my friend who was taught racial slurs, but once your mind is open you will see things truthfully. He was able to decide for himself to be my friend. You can learn things you may not have been exposed to through your family--like proper behavior at a fine dining restaurant--by paying attention. Watch the people around you and use the fork they use. And if all else fails, Google it.

Knowledge

I have been out of school for twenty years, and my kids are at an age where their homework is getting too difficult for me. I have forgotten the math formulas and such, so they cannot always rely on me for help. They have to ask a teacher or each other. The younger will ask the older sibling. We as parents do not know everything. I know you kids want us to, but we don't. Today you can find information everywhere. I have said before that everything you want to know, someone has probably written a book on the matter. Use the internet, other family members, or a class. I have taken community education classes, church classes, classes through the library, even little home groups with friends, on every topic from sign language, to cooking, to drumming. There are many things available if you take the time to find them.

Families are complicated.

Everyone's is different, but we all have some common ground. Once we have asked God into our lives, we become a part of a new family. We love our earthly family, but we get an even bigger family.

My parents are not from Minnesota. I have no extended family here, no aunts, uncles, grandparents. Until my parents each remarried and I got a wonderful group of step-brothers and sisters it was one sister, one brother, Mom, Dad and me. My husband has none of his family here in Minnesota. We have to open our hearts responsibly to others. My parents brought a church family into our lives. My husband and I have met good friends who we have been able to love like brothers and sisters.

I say "responsibly" because joining a gang, or getting pregnant, or getting into a crazy relationship is not responsible. My best friend when I was growing up lived across the alley from me. She spent every waking minute of her days at our house because being at home was not the greatest. Even Santa and the Easter Bunny found her at our house. Today, I still love her like a sister. That is God getting you what you need.

"Therefore I tell you, do not worry about your life, what will you eat or drink; or about your body, what you will wear. Is not life more important than food, and the body more important than clothes? Look at the birds of the air; they do not sow or reap or store away in barns, and yet your heavenly father feeds them are you not much more valuable than they? And why do you worry about clothes? See how the lilies of the field grow. They do not labor or spin yet I tell you that not even Solomon in all his splendor was dressed

like one of these. If that is how God clothes the grass of the field which is here today and tomorrow thrown into the fire, will he not much more cloth you?" (Matthew 6:25-28)

NOTE: If you are experiencing abuse in your home of any kind, such as physical or sexual abuse, please find a safe person to tell. A safe family member, doctor, teacher, church leader, a friend's mom, police officer, call an abuse hotline. And if you do not get the response you need, then tell someone else. But please keep telling.

5

Life as a Christian Teen

*W*hat does it mean to be a Christian? How should you live a Christian life as a teenager with so much pulling you away?

> *"Do not conform any longer to the patterns of this world, but be transformed by the renewing of your mind. Then you will be able to test and approve what God's will is-his good, pleasing, and perfect will"* (Romans 12:2).

> *"Simon, Simon, Satan has asked to sift you as wheat but I have prayed for you Simon that your faith may not fail and when you have turned back strengthened your brothers"* (Luke 22:31-32).

"Brothers think of what you were when you were called; not many of you were wise by human standards; not many of you were influential; not many were of noble birth. But God has chosen foolish things of the world to put to shame the wise; God chose the weak things of the world to put to shame the strong. He chose the lowly things of this world and the despised things--and the things that are not--to nullify the things that are, so that no one may boast before him. It is because of him that you are in Christ Jesus, who has become for us wisdom from God" (1 Corinthians 1:26-30).

What is Christianity and Religion?

Christianity can often be confused with religion and church participation. Both are important but very different. Christianity goes far beyond going to church; it is not defined by church attendance at all. Christianity is learning about God, building your personal relationship with God, and discovering the gifts God has given to you.

Religion focuses on rules and a future in heaven; Christianity focuses on how to live with God today and how to take others with you to heaven in the future.

Who is God?

1. God the Father in love He predestined us to be adopted as his sons through Jesus Christ(Ephesians 1:3-14).

2. God the Son (Romans 5:6-10).

3. God the Holy Spirit- Nor will people say, here it is, or there it is, because the kingdom of God is within you. (Ephesians 1:13-14, Luke 17:21).

How do I know God?

1. Through His word,
2. Through His promises, and
3. Through results.

There is a great account in 1 Kings 18:19-45 where Elijah, a prophet of God, calls out about 800 prophets of idols to a challenge: *"Get two bulls for us. Let them choose one for themselves, and let them cut it into pieces and put it on the wood but do not set fire to it. I will prepare the other bull and put it on the wood but not set fire to it. Then you call on the name of your god, and I will call on the name of The Lord. The god who answers by fire--he is God."* You will know it is God by the results (full account 1 Kings 18:19-45).

God is not the Church

Church is a very important part of our growth. Church is a teaching place, a place to gather with other believers. A place to draw strength from those who are farther along than you and a place to stand with other believers.

Where two or three gather in my name there I am.

I accepted God into my life, now what?

Starting your walk with God can be such an exciting time in your life. Shooting out of the gates on fire for God and excited about all the new things you are learning and experiencing, is a common thing. And wanting to share your new joy is understandable. Unfortunately those around you may not get excited about your new direction in life. You will see questions in people close to you and who shared your past life. Jesus was rejected throughout his life.

Jesus faced constant opposition from people who know his past. *They asked, "Nazareth can anything good come out of Nazareth?" (John 1:46). They replied are you from Galilee, too? Look into it, and you will find that a prophet does not come out of Galilee. (John 7:52). No prophet is accepted in his own hometown (Luke 4:24).* His own people after his message wanted to throw him off the edge of a cliff *(Luke 4:28-29).* This is just a few scriptures of many. People rejected Jesus and his disciples because their teaching and lifestyle challenged them, their popularity and their knowledge.

Success and Failure

What is true failure? Is failure bad?

"Blessed is the man who perseveres under trial, because when he has stood the test he will receive the crown of life that God has promised to those who love him." (James 1:12).

Who determines failure?

"God has chosen the foolish things of the world to put to shame the things that are mighty..." (1 Corinthians 1:27-29), "who is wise and understanding among you? Let him show it by good life, his deeds done in humility that comes from wisdom" (James 3:13). In other words, someone who is walking the walk.

What is success?

When you reach success, then what? What happens next when the team wins the final game and the season is over (when you except Christ into your life)? Is the success over? Is that all there is? We all know the old timer that ran in the winning touchdown in his younger years and still talks about it 20 years later like it happened yesterday. They will always be the winner of the game. You will always have God.

The question now becomes what have they done with that success? Are they working with new players and teaching them how to run in winning touchdowns? Are they sitting on the sidelines fussing and making others feel bad for dropping the ball? Or not even at the game but sitting at home telling their story over and over? Success is not allowing yourself to get stuck in that great victory or that first moment you got saved. Instead it is setting new goals, new targets, and getting new successes in your life. (Those old timers need the "next big touchdown").

It takes a lot of focus to excel at something. A sport can consume your focus and your time, and when you put so much into that and then the season is done, you have a lot of free time on your hands. That is the true issue with those old timers -- they did not focus on the next steps. We are quickly defeated in life because the first time we meet adversity we rush back to what is comfortable. Those old timers are comfortable where they are; that was the time in their lives they felt success. True failure is repeating the same thing over and over getting nowhere.

When people first start their relationship with God, they do not fully let go of their old ways. As a new Christian, the life style can seem unreachable. When things get tough and the warm and fuzzy wears off if your not fully committed it is easy to go back to your old ways. If you do not fully commit your life, then it does not seem like such big a fall if you quit. This can happen after you have been saved because there is so much joy, excitement, and emotion in the beginning, but after a while the focus has to change from the emotion and celebration to goals for how you are going to live a Christian life.

What does it mean to be tested?

Does this mean that God is tempting me to sin? We live in a world filled with temptations. God is not tempting us to sin, the temptations are already there. Once you choose to accept Christ into your life, things that you may have done without great thought before will become more sensitive.. Now you need to see these temptations differently.

1. Testing will show you what is truly in your heart.
2. Testing is a learning tool.

For us thick-headed folks, testing is needed as a more in-your-face way to learn.

I have a mouth problem, mainly gossip -- I love to hear it and speak it. I pray to God to help me. I read scripture books on the topic (Joyce Meyers has a good one) and read Bible scriptures (and there are a lot on this topic), but I never used that information to make changes.

It seemed like everywhere I went people came to me with juicy gossip. Was God setting me up to fail? In the beginning, I thought He was. Then He showed me that I have a reputation that I created for being a gossip. It is not a new thing to have people come to me with news. But now I am more sensitive to it.

God is not going to wave a magic wound and remove the gossip from my life. He gave me the tools through the books and the scriptures to make the changes and through prayer opened my eyes and made me sensitive to it. Now when I start to gossip, I get a pinch in my stomach (that is my Holy Spirit spot) giving me a choice to stop and walk away or ignore and continue to gossip. That is testing. Each time an opportunity to gossip comes my way it is practice, and eventually I will master it.

How do you fix a "failure"?

By doing something else, do something different. Making mistakes is unavoidable. I convinced myself that listening to gossip was not bad; it was repeating what I had heard that was bad. That was my way around what I knew to be right so I could stay in the gossip loop. Instead of entertaining the gossip, now I steer the conversation elsewhere or remove myself altogether.

Your test will become your testimony

My gossiping has hurt people. I have spread gossip told to me by others that was not true. I have shared things people told me in confidence. I have had hurtful things said about me. And I am sad about relationships I have lost and others I missed out on because of something someone said about that person keeping me away. I gossip to make myself feel better. Thanks to God showing me these things, I now have a testimony, a lesson I can pass on to you.

Who's teaching you?

"A student is not above his teacher, but everyone who is fully trained will be like his teacher" (Luke 6:40). I was raised in a church going family, so I relied on my parents' knowledge of God, and what I heard in church. When you accept Christ into your life it is the time for you to take responsibility for your relationship with God.

How will you know that you need to grow? God will make you restless, and you will feel stale. Bored, you will start to feel that there is more for you. God will stir up a hunger in your spirit. When I started my walk I read a lot of books. I would pray in the car before I went into the bookstore, asking God to help me find the perfect book. I always read books that were scripture-filled and on a topic I needed.

When I had my son I read parenting books. I have read books on the mind, the mouth, faith, forgiveness, Bible study books. There is a book on everything. These books are broken down into age groups. I wrote this book with a lot of scripture in it, not to show how smart I am but because it was very important to me in the beginning of my walk. I do not recommend that you pick up a King James Bible and start your first bible reading from Genesis through Revelations, unless that is what you feel lead to do.

I eventually read the Bible front to back (I used a "Bible in a year" guide in the back of my bible, and it took me a little over a year.) Bible reading is very important to your spiritual growth. Scriptures are taken out of context and misused to make points on a regular basis, and if you are unfamiliar with the scriptures you may not realize you are being misled. How do you know if a word is from God? *"How can we know when a message has not been spoken by the Lord? If what a prophet proclaims in the name of the Lord does not take place or come true, that is a message the Lord has not spoken". (Deuteronomy 18:21-22).*

When you get some scripture inside of you it will shock you. When you are in need God will pull that scripture out of you. You may have forgotten all about it or did not even know you knew it. But it will always show up when you need it.

Some Great Tools

Study bibles are great; my daughter has one geared toward teen girls.

Promise books are a must have; these are scripture books on the promises of God.

When you read a book that has blessed you, look in the references. Authors will list the books that they referenced, giving you more reading options. But the best resource can be the church.

What is fun?

The misconception of "fun" has left many new believers in a pickle. It is considered boring to be "good;" "bad" is considered much more fun.

Boredom is an attack on the mind. The need to avoid boredom by any means, or the idea that the more reckless the action, the more fun it is, is a dangerous mindset. Recklessness is like a drug: you have to keep upping the ante to get a charge.

When you remove something from your life you leave a space that will be filled by something else. Example: on breaks from school, weekends, holidays and summer you fill the eight hours you were in school with other activities. Sleep, sports, TV, friends, family vacations, etc. The goal is to remove the less desirable things and replace those with more desirable things.

If you draw a box on a piece of paper and you make sections in that box, some example of the sections would be, boyfriend/ friends/ school/church/ family/ me/ activities/ anything that takes your time.

If you find that you cannot fit all the things that are demanding your time in your box, things will need to be dropped. If your box is not full enough you may need to add. Filling your box does not always mean filling it with activities. Over-scheduling can be misused as a way to hide from life, and emptiness can lead to poor choices and basic laziness.

Ideas that I find to be Good Fillers

Me Time – Spend time everyday doing things for you, paint your nails, listen to music, write, read, or fix your hair. Your time is non-negotiable. So many people have trouble being alone. If this is something you struggle with, then "me time" is also your training to get past it. You cannot rely on others to entertain you for your entire life. "Me time" does not have to be deep. There needs to be a time when you quiet your mind and reboot every day.

- Watch a movie(not a heavy movie)
- Read a book
- Turn off the phone

- Stop the thoughts of the day
- Breath/exercise
- Draw

The point is to release the craziness of the day and quiet your mind for a few minutes.

Activities are not always sports. I am not an athletic person and have not found a sport I want to play. So I look for other activities, like cooking, a job, dance, playing an instrument, singing, and book club.

School – Do not forget school. This time is also non-negotiable. Skipping class to do other things is unacceptable.

How this time is divided will depend on the task. School is something you cannot control, so many hours must be spent in the classroom and so many on homework. If you have extra homework one night, time with friends may have to wait until the weekend.

If one task in the box starts to spill over into another area, you must control your borders. If your friends want in on your "me time" and arrive unannounced to hang, your job is creeping into your homework time. Activities creep into all areas. When this happens, you have to pick the ones you like best and let the others go. With the extra time, you can improve on the activities you enjoy the most.

Gifts and Talents

Can God really use me? As you study your Bible you will find that God used all kinds of unexpected people and things, He even spoke through a donkey (Numbers 22:21-31). He gave each one of us a gift. A gift to develop for his kingdom. Discovering and developing the gifts God has given you should be a big focus in your Christian walk.

What is a gift and talent?

Why did God give me gifts and talents? Why are they important? All of us have things that we are good at. It can take great thought to discover what they are, because we are programmed to focus on our shortcomings. Those shortcomings tend to get all the attention. But a life lived without using your gifts is a life lived below your potential.

Many adults go through life unhappy with their jobs, their personal lives, and their Christian lives, because they are not living in a way that uses and develops their gifts and talents. I have three kids I must feed, and a writing career is not a career that I can start and begin making a good living. Thus the term "starving artist." You have to paint the portrait before you can sell it. So I had to find something else I enjoyed while I wrote on the side. Most people would quit the gift to focus on the necessity. I say, use the necessity to develop the gift.

People who are successful are not necessarily those with the higher IQ instead they are the people who know who they are and what they are good at.

Do you know your talents and strengths?
Do you know the difference?

Talents are traits that can be developed, practiced, read, or learned from a teacher. You can train yourself. You have control over your strengths. Just because you were not born with a certain trait does not mean you cannot develop it.

Gifts are abilities preprogrammed inside of you, such as to sing, to play ball, to write, to work with people, to organize, to plan, a gift to be a caregiver... You do not have control over your gifts. I am not a singer. I can get a vocal coach, practice and even imitate other singers, but I can only be so good at it. I also fall short in the gift of organization -- I buy boxes, watch shows on HGTV, and label things but it only gets me so far. Do you know what your gifts are?

I think about what I enjoy and what comes easily to me, what I do when I lose myself and look up and hours went by. Those are your clues. I am a writer; give me a pen and paper and words just pour out on the page. I have scraps of paper everywhere. I am also very clever, which helps me be creative when I write and quickly come up with ideas.

For some, discovering your gifts will be easy. Others may get distracted on what you want your gifts to be. There is a woman at church who REALLY has a gift to clean. She has been cleaning the church behind the scenes for years. She gets no awards for what she does and I do not think members of the church even think about the cleaning crew. But, without knowing, they enjoy the beautiful atmosphere in the building week after week. This lady could turn away from her gift to pursue a more desirable gift, like a ministry leader. We can get hung up on the "popular gifts" and feel as though our gift is not good enough. For example, I Googled top-paying dirty jobs. On that list: Portable toilet cleaner, Sewer inspector, and a Gastroenterologist (Butt Doctor). God has spread the gifts around so every task is covered, "popular" or not.

Some people will be confused and get wrapped up in talents that distract from their gift. I am good at a lot of things. When my kids were little, I learned how to decorate cakes because specialty cakes came from bakeries and were not found in every grocery store. They were quite expensive. Ryan wanted a Lion King cake for his birthday so I spent SEVERAL hours decorating this cake for him and it turned out fantastic! (A stranger at the place we had his party tried to buy it from me.) It took forever to make, my hands cramped up from squeezing the piping bag and shortly after presenting the cake everyone was asking "when are we cutting the cake?" Hours of work for minutes of pleasure.

I made all my kids' cakes and every time they got more impressive. People would offer to buy cakes from me and I did sell a few, but I honestly hated making them. And once they got easy to buy at the grocery store, I quickly retired my piping bag.Years later, people try to get me to decorate cakes, but that was a talent and not a gift.

Your gifts will need to be polished

You will need to polish your gifts. If you are a writer, then you need to find ways to improve your writing. I said earlier that I took up more reading. If you have a gift to sing, then join a choir or take vocal lessons; or if you have a gift for dance, join the dance team, etc.

Athletics are a good example for this. You may be the star basketball player in high school and receive a college scholarship but when you get to college you sit the bench your whole first season. You need to prepare for the next level. When you become a college star you may get recruited to play on a professional team and again not see any playing time until you are prepared for that level. After you have completed your career as a gifted player, you have to prepare for that level as well.

People may not be supportive of the gifts God gave you.

My daughter is very artistic. She is always dragging what I consider junk home, which bothers me because I do not see her vision -- I see trash in my house. There was a time that she cut the center out of her bed sheets for the fabric to make a purse. I cannot understand her gift because it is hers.

My son Nathan is a great storyteller. I get irritated with his gift for a different reason. He is just like me, and I want that talking time.

My oldest son Ryan is a poet. Poetry is very personal, and I have to not take his writing personally and remember that emotions can be transformed to create a piece.

It would be easy for me to squash my kids with punishments and belittling, or to refuse to allow my daughter to work on her art projects, or to reject my son's poetry because I read too much into it and I got offended. And my children could allow my response to change the way they respond to their gifts. God gave them these gifts, and they are required to use them. This does not mean she can keep cutting holes in her sheets.

What an insult to God to waste a gift he has given you. *Do not get caught up in what you think to be important (Galatians 2:6).*

6

So my words that go out of my mouth: will not return to me empty, but will accomplish what I desire and achieve the purpose for which I sent them.

Your quality of life is directly affected by your mouth.

The opening verse says, "My words will not return to me empty." It says MY words. Not my mom's words, my peers' words, or my boyfriend's words, but MY words. The good words as well as the bad. Have you ever entered a contest and said before the results were released, "I never win anything?" Or made a mistake and said, "I'm so stupid" or a friend told a joke and in laughter said, "stop it you're killing me"? These are just a few of the common things we say without thought of their power.

The bible has a lot of scriptures on the power of the tongue. Bookstore shelves are heavy with books written on the power of words, both positive spoken words and negative. The reason for this is having a solid understanding on how powerful your mouth is and how your words will affect your life and those around you, could be the piece that is missing in your life.

People will treat you the way you tell them to.

Every time you say something bad about yourself it gives others permission to do the same. You tell people things every time you open your mouth. It is not direct, like, "treat me badly please" but indirect. I hear people say terrible things about themselves without any thought. I have heard many women when they make a mistake say "that was my blond moment." Or introduce themselves as "just me." Or the one that "drives me crazy" is when we point out flaws no one else is even concerned with. We have all instructed someone taking our picture to "take my good side" or "don't use that one, it shows my fat chin or big nose...."

Words will affect your environment.

Being surrounded by negativity can have a major effect on you. Negative words can shift the direction God has for your life. If you are told you will never amount to anything, you may achieve things in your life, but that voice can haunt you.

I was told REPEATEDLY that my brother was the smart one. He achieved many great things academically in high school, he went to MIT for college, and returned to school to receive a master's degree. I successfully under-achieved in high school, went to college at a school that was nationally ranked as one of the top party schools, and completed three years. Every time I do something (like write a book) I am reminded about how my brother is "the smart one." This could have held me back from trying anything academic. I had to learn to turn that voice in my head off and tell myself what I can and cannot do.

A successful mouth

Displays integrity, trustworthiness, respect for self and others, unselfishness, humility, self-discipline, self-control and courage. Wow, this is a tough list. But each one of these traits are goals. None of us are perfect, but if we focus on the plan God has for us and go through life doing the best we can, also speaking the best words possible in all situations, we will see growth.

Your wisdom will be evaluated by the way you speak.

All spoke well of him and were amazed at the gracious words that came from his lips. "Isn't that Joseph's son?" they asked (Luke 4:22.) In this verse they could not believe a carpenter's son could be so well-spoken. In the same way, they judged Jesus for being a carpenter's son. People will judge you on the way you speak.

As a teenager, your message can be judged because it will not be coming from a source the hearers expect. *"Do not worry about what to say or how to say it at that time you will be given what to say, for it will not be you speaking, but the spirit of your father speaking through you" (Matthew 10:19-20).*

Words are the way we communicate. Sometimes, saying the right thing at the right time can leave us speechless. That is the great thing about this verse: when you need the right words, God will help.

Prayer: The best use of our words

What other nation is so great as to have their gods near them the way The Lord our God is near us whenever we pray to him?(Deuteronomy 4:7)

We can get caught up in prayer rituals that can distract us from the purpose of what we are doing, like the idea that you have to be on your knees, that you have to pray for a certain amount of time every day, that your prayers have to be insightful, poetic, or highly educated. You are missing out on the point of prayer, which is to have a conversation with God, to be near to Him. This is the cornerstone to your relationship.

Prayer is not a wish list for Santa Claus or time spent begging for forgiveness for all the terrible things you did. Prayer is a balanced conversation between you and God. I say balanced because there should be time to speak and time to listen.

A place to start: Prayer is a personal thing, but there should be some guidelines, just to keep on track.

Worship: What is worship, and why does God need me to worship Him? We worship our favorite celebrities, we worship things, we worship money, and we even worship ourselves. Worshipping God redirects focus that we are putting on other things back where it belongs.

Forgiveness: God knows what I did, why do I have to ask for forgiveness? When you ask forgiveness from your heart and are truly genuine about it, it is not for God but for you. I have used the word "focus" so many times in this book that I really thought about trying not to use it again, but prayer gives you focus. If I am asking God to forgive me for the same thing over and over again (which I have done) after a while it clicks within me: I have not been serious about it. We have a loving and forgiving God. We try to take advantage of that forgiveness by willingly sinning with the idea that all we have to do is ask for forgiveness and all will be well.

Ask: We get so discouraged in this area. The Bible says *"I tell you the truth, my Father will give you whatever you ask in my name. Until now you have not asked for anything in my name. Ask and you will receive, and your joy will be complete."(John 16:23-24)* The part we all overlook is that those requests need to be scriptural and in line with God's plan for you.

If you are irresponsible with your money and pray and pray for God to rescue you, you will not be able to pay your rent if He does not. When God does not put a sack of cash on your front step, and you get evicted can you get upset with God?

What are some things to ask for? *Do not be anxious about anything but in everything, by prayer and petition, with thanksgiving present your request to God.*

I am in no way saying not to ask for your needs to be met, but add a bit more to your prayers than just material things.

1. -Pray that you will not fall into temptation *(Luke 22:40)*.

2. -Pray for understanding *(Ephesians 6:18-20)*.

3. -Pray for those who persecute you *(Matthew 5:44, Luke 6:28)*.

4. -Pray for the strength to forgive others *(Mark 11:24-25)*.

5. -Pray that God's will be done not your will *(Luke 22:42)*.

6. -And pray for it all in Jesus' name (Colossians 3:17).

Give thanks: *Be joyful always; pray continually; give thanks in ALL circumstances for this is God's will for you in Christ Jesus (1Thessalonians 5:16-18)*. Does God really mean *all* circumstances? Even the bad ones? All is all. How can you possibly be thankful in a bad circumstance? The best way is to learn from it. We all face tough stops in our lives and make mistakes. When, not if, you make it through those times and you have grown, they can be rewarding lessons. It is hard to see in the moment, but once you are on the other side you will see.

I mentioned how my first "true love" treated me horribly. Am I thankful for how he did me wrong? Heck no. But I learned a valuable lesson, exactly what I do not want in a man. Because of this relationship, I am married to a great man and father.

I am thankful that God saw me through, I am thankful for the lesson I learned, and I am thankful for the growth I received. It sounds like spiritual chatter but it is true. You can be thankful in all circumstances.

I recently took a job even though I felt God was prompting me to stay home to take care of my family. This job had a nice title, I had business cards to pass out, the money was a real perk for the family, and my pride wanted the status. I did not want to be "just a housewife".

I was hired for this dream job that I had wanted so badly. It turned out to be the worst work environment I have ever been in. I was so stressed that I ended up having health problems; I was tired and cranky all the time. By the end I hated every part of the day. I started hating the next day before the current day had ended. During it all, I prayed earnestly for God to make it better. I finally cried out to God, asking him why he had abandoned me. The response I got was, "it's not blessed because I never told you to take this job." I was reminded of the promptings God had given me before to stay home and care for my family.

Just to guarantee the message sunk in, I was shown how unavailable I was for my family, and how little caring I was doing. Ouch, talk about hurt feelings. The company was sold shortly after this and I was laid off. Laid off sounds bad, right?

But I was so thankful to be free from that place and thankful for the lesson I learned. The lesson: If you decide to go it alone and step away from what God has for you, then it is your mess to manage. God was there to offer me respectful ways out but my pride kept refusing until I was so thankful for that final out he offered. In that moment of loss, I felt incredibly blessed. That is how you stay thankful in ALL circumstances, by learning and being grateful for how God gets you through. Even those messes you created for yourself.

What do you do when you do not know what to say?

Prayer can be as simple as:

1. God, I need you.
2. Thank you God.

3. I have found myself with no words. I laughed aloud in amazement when God made a way for me.

4. I have just lifted my hands to heaven.

Speak the Word

There is overwhelming power in speaking the word of God, quoting scripture. The Bible has scriptures for everything you need in life. How do you find those scriptures? When I started my walk someone gave me a promise book. It is a book of scriptures on the Promises of God. You can also find scriptures quickly in the back of your Bible.

The best is when you are in need and the Holy Spirit will put a scripture in your heart. It could be one you heard years ago in Sunday school or one your parents used to say. Or when you do not know where it came from but it is the perfect scripture for that moment.

Keeping a journal as you read your Bible to write scriptures is a tool every Christian needs. Even if the verse is not for that moment, when the moment comes you will be ready.

Speaking in Tongues

"The same way the Spirit helps us in our weakness. We do not know what to pray for but the Spirit himself intercedes for us with groans that words cannot express"(Romans 8:26).

Speaking in tongues can seem strange if you do not understand what is happening. Not all of us were given a gift for public speaking, and we hear our church leaders pray eloquently and with power and feel that the words we stumble over are not good enough or that they will not be answered. Sometimes you cannot put together the words.

Speaking in tongues is making sounds with your heart open to the Holy Spirit, speaking for you. You will feel silly at first, even if you are in your room alone. Simply said, get over it. God knows your heart, do the best you can and trust that God got it right.

1. -Hear my prayer o Lord listen to my cry for mercy. In the day of my trouble I will call to you for you will answer me. (Psalms 86:6-7).

2. -Their prayers reached heaven (2 Chronicles 30:27).

3. -The Lord accepts my prayer (Psalms 6:9).

7

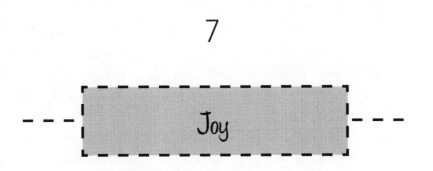

Do not grieve; the Joy of the Lord is your strength. Joy is not something we have to search for; it's already in you.

There are so many unhappy teenagers that I would like to touch on depression. I want to discuss my experience, because I am not an expert in this field.

> **Depression**: a state of being depressed: as a pressing down, lowering. A state of feeling sad: dejected. Marked also by sadness, inactivity, difficulty in thinking and concentration, a significant increase or decrease in appetite and time spent sleeping, feelings of dejection and hopelessness, and in some cases suicidal thoughts or wishing to die.

Joy: the emotion evoked by well-being, success, or good fortune or by the prospect of possessing what one desires: delight.

I like the second half of this definition, because it reminds me that I can have joy in the prospect of what I want. Or before I actually get it.

Our focus as Christians should be to live a life opposite of depression, a life of peace and joy. In the back of your Bible there is a concordance; if you use that concordance to look up the word "joy" it will show you everywhere in the Bible the word "joy" is used. In my NIV bible the word "joy" is listed 64 times, and "peace" is found 57 times.

Peace and joy are vital to living a full, Godly life. The mission for us all is to face what I call "joy stealers." What are the joy stealers in your life? They could be endless but I have picked a few that seem to effect a lot of us.

Not taking responsibility for your own joy.

We are so willing to give away our joy. We have all heard the saying "misery loves company." Well, the people that you surround yourself with can be some of the biggest joy stealers out there. When you have something good happen to you, perhaps you did well on a test, but then you have a friend in the class who did not do so well. The joy stealer occurs when you turn away from the joy you have about how well you did to console your friend.

Our emotions.

Learning to control your emotions is a life-long process. I am a very impatient person. If only the world would move at my pace I would be just fine, but it never seems to work like that. I was at a Target store on a very busy day. When I got in line to check out, the cashier needed assistance and turned on the flashing light. I instantly got upset. I started thinking "every time I come to this store I pick the lines that have the problems." (This thought is a joy stealer). All the lines were backed up, so switching was not going to get me out any faster. After a few minutes I decided not to give away my joy to this.

The person in front of me responsible for the flashing light became very stressed, looked at me, and said, "I'm so sorry." I smiled and said "No problem." Her shoulders relaxed; she was a little red in the face and that started to fade. We both left the store with our joy. I could have given in to my feelings and given this woman all kinds of attitude. Instead, I controlled my emotions and was able to add joy to myself and her.

How do I regain my joy after a slip? By making some changes.

CHANGE YOUR MIND. I heard a pastor once say "I think myself Happy." My thoughts are the joy stealers in my life. Every negative thought can be changed to a positive one.

1. I am valuable.
2. God loves me.
3. I am not responsible for others.
4. I am not a quitter.

CHANGE YOUR ACTIONS. My behaviors are the joy stealers in my life.

1. Back-talking my parents.
2. Not performing in school.
3. Bullying.
4. Boyfriend.

CHANGE MY WORDS. The things I say are the joy stealers in my life. What I say about myself has more power than anything someone else says about me.

1. I will no longer say negative things about myself.
2. I will not accept negative words others say about me.
3. I will not accept the negative words and images the media say about me.
4. I love who I am right now.

Once you remove one of the joy stealers in your way, you need to replace it with something else. Remember our definition of Joy at the start of this chapter? Part of that definition is having well-being and success. Success is not just the end results but the steps you take to get there. We make success into such a big word, which only focuses on the end product, which can be frustrating when it's a long road ahead. We can miss that each step, no matter how small, that moves us closer to the goal: is success. So what are some successful steps closer to joy?

Help others. Helping others is a great way to add joy to your life, because it distracts you from focusing on yourself. This is an area where people think way too big at times. People feel that to help others they have to start a world-wide foundation, go on a mission trip to a third world country or raise large quantities of money (if that is your calling, that is great). Helping others can also be holding the door open for a mom whose hands are full at the mall, helping a classmate pick up books dropped in the hall (instead of laughing), mentoring a younger sister, volunteering at the humane society, or helping an environmental group clean the local beaches. You do not have to help just people -- sometimes a break from people is a good thing.

Clean your room. A clean space can help quiet your mind.

Get a job and perform well on that job. Babysit, and while babysitting read to the kids or play games with them instead of talking on the phone all night or sitting the kids in front of the TV. Wash the dinner dishes the parents left behind, leaving the house better than when you got there. Do not expect to be paid more or praised for it; if they offer it, great, but do it for you not them.

Make a new friend. The easiest way to strike up a conversation with someone is to smile and say "hi" then ask that person something about him or herself: "I saw you reading ABC book I was thinking about reading it also, what did you think about it?"

Learn something new. This is not the time to sign up for piano lessons if you know that if you are not playing like a professional in a week you will be discouraged. To avoid discouragement, start small. Get a friend to teach you how to French braid. Print off a recipe you wanted your mom to make and ask her to teach you how to make it. Go online and get the word of the day or a quotation of the day.

Watch one less hour of TV and read a book. It's not as much about the book as it is about the stillness.

Be grateful. Gratitude is a very healing. The Bible speaks a lot about gratitude or being thankful. Not because God needs his ego stroked but because it is very uplifting for us. Being thankful, for not just the obvious things -- "thank you God for this food" -- but also the not so obvious things as well. Be thankful for the cloudy, rainy day because the rain just washed away the leaves your mom wanted you to rake. Or the traffic on the way to school because you forgot to finish an assignment and now have more time on the bus to finish. Be thankful you did not make the team because you were joining for the wrong reasons and you really need that time to focus on your schoolwork.

It Takes a Commitment to:

Pay attention. When I was in line at Target I had to pay attention to the feelings rising up in me.

Make adjustments. You cannot remove all the joy stealers in your life, but you can make the necessary adjustments to deal with them differently. If your friend failed the test and is stealing your joy of doing well, do not join her pity party. Break away and be proud of what you have done and catch up with her later.

Fake it until you make it. You may be going crazy inside but if you do not give in that crazy feeling will pass. When I was in line at Target, I may have smiled and said "no problem" but I was not feeling all that joyful. The impatient feeling did quickly pass. DO NOT go to the car after you just saved your joy and unload on your friends: "Can you believe that lady in front of us?" This will steal the joy you just created. Also, keep your friends in check and remind them that we have all picked the shirt that was missing the tag. And drop it.

The depression I am speaking about in this chapter is a level of sadness that dims your mood day to day. I am not a mental health expert and do not know the ins and outs of depression. Any of the feelings listed in the definition at the beginning of this chapter, especially suicidal thoughts, require that you find help. Tell a parent, school counselor -- high schools where I am from have clinics in them -- speaking to your doctor, pastor or youth leader, or going online and finding a hotline. You must tell someone, even if you can only write a sentence on a scrap of paper that says, "I'm unhappy and I don't know why" and hand it to a trustworthy adult.

In this chapter I have tips that I used in my own life and they have worked for me in times of sadness. There may be things that are going on in your life that you feel no one will understand. You might not understand. Start by talking out loud to yourself privately; sometimes the hardest part is putting words to the feelings. Once you have put the words together you must find a trustworthy adult. This is not for your peers.

1. I am feeling sad. I cry all the time and I don't know why.

2. I have feelings of hurting myself or others.

3. I am always angry.

4. Someone is hurting me physically, sexually, or mentally.

You do not have to understand why, you just need the words. If you cannot speak them, write them down in a letter and give that letter to that trustworthy adult. The letter does not need to be a grand essay but whatever you can put together. It may only say "I'm hurting," and that is enough.

Fear of how that person you tell will respond can be paralyzing -- just remember the opening scripture *"the joy of the Lord is your strength."* If you do not get the response that you need, pick yourself up and go to someone else.

Some people respond to things negatively because they do not understand how to deal with the situation. Just remember that is their issue, not yours. *"The thief does not come except to steal, and kill, and destroy. I have come that they may have life, and that they may have it more abundantly " (John 10:10).*

8

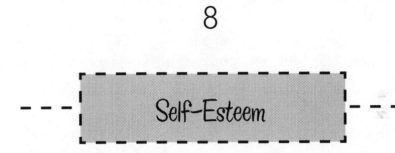

Self-Esteem

A new life with God will change our attitude, motives, values, and will.

What is self-esteem?

Self-esteem is a phrase that is tossed around and blamed for everything. Do you really know what it means? I like to look at the words separately: Self, meaning you, and esteem, meaning to set a high value on; regard highly; prize accordingly.

So it is your job to "set a high value on," "regard highly," and my favorite of the definitions, "prize accordingly," yourself. It is vital that you remember this because the way you esteem (value) yourself will directly affect your attitude, motives, value, and willingness.

What is your esteem saying?

Your esteem sends out messages to all those around you, telling them how to treat you. To recognize some of the messages your esteem is sending out, spend a week taking journal notes on how people are treating you. How do they speak to you? Are you lifted up or torn down? In the same week, journal about how you treat yourself. How do I speak to myself? Do I lift myself up or tear myself down?

Why is my self-esteem important?

What does it matter how I feel about myself? If your self-esteem is low then you will live a low life. You will stay stuck, convincing yourself you are not worthy of growth.

Self-esteem affects how you treat yourself. Low esteem will make it okay for you to punish yourself as in drug use, abusive relationships, or self-sabotage. We may physically hurt or mentally hurt ourselves (taking risks, smoking, not eating, eating too much. Or saying I'm so stupid, fat, ugly, etc.)

We wear our self-esteem like a badge. It is our message that we consciously and unconsciously send out to the people around us, like radio waves telling them how to treat us.

Teachers can overlook a kid with little confidence. A shy, quiet kid can become invisible in a classroom. Teachers tend to engage kids they know will respond, to keep the discussion moving. They are not trying to be hurtful; they cannot spend every day dragging someone out of their shell.

Confidence (which is the product of good self-esteem) weighs heavily in your peer groups, from who you will be friends with, to what power they will or will not have over you.

Boys are going to treat a girl with a high self-esteem differently than a girl with a low self-esteem. They are not calling the girls with high self-esteem names, they are not using the girls with high self-esteem for sex or whatever else they can get. And they surely are not hitting or hurting those girls.

Even animals can pick out the weak. When a lion is stalking its prey, it lays back and evaluates the herd of antelope passing by. There could be hundreds, but that lion can pick the one it has the best chance to overpower. That lion will concentrate everything on that weak antelope. That is the one who will be dinner.

Why do some people have high self-esteem and others low?

The answer to this question is endless. Every person has a different story. I have a pretty good image of myself. I always have. I did allow distractions such as media, my peers, and boys to creep in during periods of my young life, but I have always bounced back. There are many reasons for this. One reason is I had a family that surrounded me with people who lifted me up. People from our church family, great God parents, my mom's sewing club. If my feelings got hurt in one area, or if my mom or dad did not respond in a way I needed, there was always someone else to step in. As I got older, I studied by reading books, reading my bible. I visualized what I wanted in my life and studied how to get it. The "self" side of esteem.

There are those who feel that they are going it alone, that no one is there for them. No one is going to step in and lift me up like that Priscilla. That may be true, and that is why it is called SELF esteem. Not Momma or Daddy esteem, not Peer esteem, and not Boyfriend esteem. People cannot lift you up higher than where they are. You are responsible for your Self-esteem.

- Remember in Chapter One when I used a scripture from Genesis, when God asked the question "who told you"? I ask you, who told you that you are not pretty enough? The media? They will tell you anything to get you to buy their product. A boy? Find another boy. Who told you that you are not smart enough? Ask for help. Read instead of watching hours of TV. Study. We have to stop giving away our power and take charge of our own mindset. People are self-serving. We do not mean to be hurtful, but we treat and speak to each other based on what we want from one another. Sometimes consciously, sometimes unconsciously.

As little girls we all knew the girl who wanted to control every game (usually the one who had the stuff). If you did not let her have her way, she would pack up her stuff and leave. Everyone knew if you wanted to keep playing with her stuff, the rule was to keep her happy. Everyone got what they wanted but both had to sacrifice, one of you has to play with someone you do not like to get the toy, the other has to use the toy to get you to play with her.

This mentality goes far past the playground. Girls use sex appeal, boys use attention. Kids exhaust themselves to over-achieve in school to gain attention from a parent. Friends hold back affection to manipulate each other to do things. I will not be your friend if you do not …..I will be your friend if you do…

These are Self Esteem driven motives. Self-esteem affects your motives. What is a motive? Motive implies an emotion or desire operating on the will and causing it to act.

In the first example, if the kid without the toy did not sell herself short for some toys, she could be playing with another kid that she actually likes. If the other girl felt that she was better than her toys, she would not need to hold them over someone to keep them around. She would hold out for a friend who wants to play with her, toy or not.

Poor self-esteem is poor value of self. The definition of value is to rate or scale in usefulness, importance or general worth.

When I was little I was given a Holly Hobby cookbook. There was one caramel recipe that I really liked and made many times, but that was it. After I had made the caramel enough times, I memorized the recipe, and the little cook book lost its value to me. Many years later, I was putting together a garage sale and decided that the Holly Hobby cookbook had to go. It was taking up space, and I had not opened it in years. I sold it for twenty-five cents. Funny thing, about a month later, I was craving that caramel sauce and decided to look the book up online. Guess what I found? That little cookbook was a collector and worth $250. I often wonder if the person who bought it laughed all the way to the bank at my ignorance.

Who gives you your value?

TV can give you value. If you act like the character on a popular show you will get value. A parent, or rather the love and validation of a parent, can give you value. Your peers or being in the "IN" crowd can give you value. Magazines, clothes, stuff. Being the first girl to have the newest Coach bag can give value. A boyfriend, grades, being part of a team, all can give you value.

What happens when the popular TV show is no more, the parent takes on a second job and becomes distracted, the peer group turns on you, basketball season comes to an end, and some other girl beats you to the next season Coach bag? You will be forced to redirect that focus to God, who gave you your value in the womb before all that other stuff.

If I had known my Holly Hobby cook book had value, I would have treated it better. I would have treated it like the $250.00 book it was. You already know your value. It is time to start treating yourself at that level, once you do everyone else will follow- Coach bag or not.

How do I raise low self-esteem?

Raising low self-esteem is tied into a lot of the same things involved in changing your image. You have to accept your value first. Then it becomes a battle for the mind and the mouth. When you make a mistake are you quick to say, "I'm so stupid". Is your mind quick to go to the negative?

I have a 17-year-old son who is driving. When he is late getting home, my first thoughts can be negative. What if he has been in an accident? I have to change my mind with the first negative thought, I squash it by saying, "thank you God for your angels who guard him and protect him all of his ways".

You are a child of God. You should never speak negatively about yourself, and you should never accept things said against you that are not in line with what God said. When you start to have negative thoughts, speak to yourself what God said. I am created in his image, everything he created is good. Keep some of those verses from Chapter One in your journal And repeat them as many times as necessary.

Changing low self-esteem is changing your mind. The focus spent on the negatives must be redirected to solutions. If you feel everyone is treating you badly, the solution is to stop letting them. Stop folding like a deck of cards to that boyfriend when he pressures you. What is the worst thing that could happen if you say no? Will he break up with you for someone who will say yes? That might happen, but if it does, he was not a good boyfriend. He was using you to get what he wanted.

If you do not like your weight, find ways to lose it. I do not mean to make these changes sound simple, because they are not, but keeping your self-esteem tied to exterior things such as peers, purses, and boyfriends will not help you. When those things are gone you will be right back where you started or may be even worse off.

Know that you have value and be determined to make the changes for the solutions you need, which sometimes requires outside help from a parent, a doctor, or a mentor. If you do not, your self-esteem may never improve.

9

Friends, And Idols

God would speak to Moses face to face as a friend,
(Exodus 33:11); A friend loves at all times, (Proverbs. 17:17)

Who are your friends?

We are social creators, and a group makes us feel that we are part of something. Hollywood does not help with this topic: every TV show and movie portraying teens puts out the message that to be popular is the only way. If you are not in the right crew or a crew at all, you are a nobody.

As children we instinctually follow to survive. We trust, obey, and follow our parents, relying on them for protection. As we get older we can still look to follow, an instinct that is in us to follow God.

Following is not limited to people. You can follow money, food, and feelings. The emotional need to fit in is a big leader in our lives; not only can it cloud your judgment, but it can make you knowingly and willingly go against what you believe to be right. So why is a social group so important?

We feel safe with our group and that outweighs the rational desire to lead. It is painful and frightening to stand up against the group, or go out alone, so most of us conform. The need to follow can outweigh good judgment and put us in danger. Your tolerance to bad behavior will move up until you find yourself in a place you never thought you would go. You try drugs, because everyone else in the group is doing it. You have sex because the group is pressuring you to join the non-virgins club.

How do you avoid going down the wrong path to be part of the group?

Not all groups are bad, in any group you have to stand up against the little wrongs before they turn into bigger ones. Not everyone has the strong leader personality, so making things clear up front is a must. "I have no plans of having sex, I will not skip class to hang out, and I am no one's soldier doing what I'm told to stay in the group." You need to understand who you are allowing to lead you. Can everyone in your group be heard? A true leader can hear others. Do your friends hear you?

What does it mean to be popular?

How many friends does that require? Do you have to be cutthroat and outright mean to be popular? Once I become popular what is required to stay there?

Every Hollywood "popular girl" crew is set up the same. There's the leader, there's second in command, and there's the soldiers. There is no real loyalty in these crews because number two wants to be number one. Number one needs to stay number one. And the soldiers need number one and number two to put them in the right social standing. The soldiers tend to do anything for number one or number two to stay in the group.

This set-up has jumped off the movie and television screens and landed in our schools and neighborhoods. I have seen this group structure in all age groups, from elementary to adult women in the workplace.

I was considered popular in school. I dated the football player; I won Homecoming Sophomore Lady and Snow Daze Queen my senior year. I had many people that I hung out with, and I was a leader. But at the end of it all I only really had one true friend, one friend who stuck closer than a sister, and we are still friends today.

The idea of popularity has gotten so out of hand that I am not sure many of us know what true friendship looks like. There were times in the middle of my "popularity" and surrounded by people that I felt lonely. I could not talk to those people, have a heart to heart, or even show my true self. At some point it would come out and be used against me. I think back on it today; it was such a waste to put so much energy into people I could not trust.

So what is true friendship?

"A man of many companion may come to ruin, but there is a friend who sticks closer than a brother". *(Proverbs. 18:24)*. The Bible gives examples of what a friendship should be

(Proverbs 17:17, Proverbs 27:6). A true friend is someone you can trust, someone that speaks to you in truth and love. Someone who can share the spot light and does not become jealous. Someone who never punishes or manipulates you. And someone who never requires things to stay your friend. The "me" becomes "we." This list is not just for you to gauge others but for you to also gauge yourself as a friend. In the hope that you will take an honest look at your situation to determine if you are someone you would want as a friend or someone God would want as a friend.

What idols are you worshiping?

The Bible is full of warnings about idols. What is an idol? It's an image or material thing that is worshiped over God. *"Come, make us gods who will go before us" he took what they handed him and made it into an idol cast into the shape of a calf.* (Paraphrased by me; the full account *Exodus 32*).

You might say, "what does that have to do with me? I have no Golden calf in my room." The question can be changed to what is commanding your attention? We live in a very materialistic world. If you do not have the right this or that you can quickly be dismissed. This is not limited to just the latest Coach bag or Ugg boots. This can be the overwhelming need to be part of the "right" group of friends or to have the "right" boyfriend. There is no harm in having things. The idol is when those things have you, or those things take your attention and begin to drive you.

I made myself an idol once. I was a person who needed the spotlight and I had a friend who had low self-esteem. She was a bit overweight and her family did not have a lot. She was the perfect sidekick for me. In my mind she never stole my spotlight. I thought I was prettier than her, I was more popular than her, and I was thinner than her. My family had more money so I had more stuff then she did, plus she needed me because being my friend got her in circles she could not get in without me. And if she ever got too big for her place, I would play the golden calf.

We would be at my house getting dressed to go out and I would put out a suggestion like this: "Why don't you try on one of these new miniskirts my mom bought me?" I knew she could not afford to have one of her own, I also knew she would not fit them. It would always put her "back in her place" and draw a compliment for me. "You know I can't fit in your skinny girl clothes." I was using myself and my things to draw worship.

We can also make "Good things" into idols, athletes, television or movie stars. Athletes and stars have been given a gift. It is okay to admire that gift, but you cannot put all your attention on it. I see young girls who want to be just like the tween stars and musicians they admire, but that takes away from who they are supposed to be.

I love the story of the way villagers humanely trap pesky monkeys. A clay jar with a neck that tapers into a larger bottom is tied to a tree. Then peanuts are placed into this "monkey jar" and the trap is set. The monkey will place his hand in the jar and try to grab the peanuts; however he cannot remove his hand as long as he holds onto the nuts. So the monkey is trapped and will remain stuck, refusing to release the peanuts to remove his hand from the jar. It is then a simple matter for the villagers to attach a leash and collar to the monkey before breaking the jar and leading him away to a more remote location.

I like this story because my first reaction was, "silly monkey just leave the peanuts behind." Until I realized how much I do this same thing in my life. I hold on to things until I have become trapped by them.

10

Boys

Young girls are being programmed to "need" a boyfriend, at any cost. The media promotes this in every form: music, television, movies, even books. This is promoted in every age group, from tween to adult. The neediness is seen sexually, mentally, fight for him, steal him from a friend, whatever needs to be done, you have to have him. I want our girls to take their power back.

Do not give dogs what is sacred; do not throw your pearls to pigs if you do, they may trample them under their feet, and then turn and tear you to pieces. (Matthew 7:6)

The disturbing images on TV and in music anger me. It is the message sent out to young girls over and over: "You must have the attention of a boy to be valuable." A "bad boy" is the one for you. He should rule over you like a king, and you should be thankful to have him. It does not matter how he treats you, hold on to him. Be thankful you have him, and never forget that you are his.

This need to keep the guy has brought on a media craze of girl fights. They are found on YouTube, rap songs have been written about them, even celebrities have been caught in "cat fights." The cattiness starts when someone even thinks to set eyes on "your man".

My daughter had a clash with a girl who confronted her about being friends with her boyfriend. (They were friends before the girlfriend). When I say clash I am cleaning it up. This girl, who my daughter did not even know, via text, told her to stop being friends with her boyfriend and went on to call her several bad names.

We girls have to stop fighting against each other and understand what a relationship should look like, and your role in it.

Men are hunters, make them hunt.

What is it that we like about "the bad boys" -- mystery, reputation, the strength? Guess what, boys want the same thing. They like girls who have some mystery. They want a girlfriend they can be proud of. They are attracted to a girl who has power in herself. Boys have little interest in a girl who can give everything about herself in the first five minutes. Some girls not only give it away but jam it down the boy's throat. That aggressive chasing is effective in getting his attention, but it will not keep his interest.

I have two teenage boys, and I asked my sons how boys talk about girls in the locker room. Ladies, it is not good.

They are telling everything they did with you (with a lot of exaggerations). Even worse, they are trading you like playing cards. If there is a boy looking to drop his virginity, the guys will suggest to him what they call a "practice girl". These are the girls with the "I'll-do-anything-for-a-boyfriend" image, even if they are not "doing anything," their actions make it hard to defend against the lies. That is why they choose them. It sounds harsh but in the same way, girls have the constant messages put on them to get that guy, the guys have messages also.

On the other hand, if a guy is talking about a girl who has a reputation as a "good girl," the other guys will call him out saying "no way man, she is out of your league, you are full of it". They defend her. I heard it from the guys themselves.

If you are spending all your time doing the chasing, or if you must go to great lengths to get a guy's attention, he is not interested. Guys like the hunt; it is their nature. You may get his attention for a while, but you will find it is not the attention that will last beyond what it is you are offering. You can fight every girl that comes his way, but it will not work. I promise you, it just feeds the guy's ego and makes you look bad.

You are not your own; you were bought at a price therefore honor God with your body " *(1 Corinthians 6:19-20)*. A price that is so much higher than the attention from a boy.

Having a boyfriend is so important to young girls.

It was to me, too. But how do you know it is the right guy? There is an idea out there that when you enter high school every girl needs to be a cheerleader and date a football player. In my son's high school there are 3,000 students. Just to make things simple, let's say that half are boys and half girls. There are roughly thirty girls on the cheerleading squad and thirty boys on the varsity football team. That means 1,470 girls will not be cheerleaders and 1,470 boys will not be football players. 2,940 of us are allowing ourselves to be influenced by sixty. That is a bit unbalanced.

Look at this from a boyfriend perspective with the media's idea that every girl should date a football player. It means each football player has fifty girls each to choose from. If you are one of the chosen girls, keeping his attention can be a constant battle. This may put you in a position where you are more likely to do whatever it takes to keep him, since if you will not do it (whatever "it" may be) there are forty-nine other girls who might. On the other side of this equation, there are 1,470 other boys who are not football players. Odds are better there. **Just a note: not all football players are going to be jerks. This is just a point to ensure you do not get stuck in this small media box.**

Males and females are hardwired differently. Females come to a relationship with different expectations. You may have no interest in dating a football player but the point is, do not get sucked into the hype.

We must have knowledge of God so we are not *carried away by Trickery of men, crafty and deceitful, plotting* (Paraphrased by me. *Ephesians 4:13-16.*).

That does not mean just boys, but media, peer pressure, and your own misconceptions. There is nothing wrong with having a boyfriend -- you just need to understand how to do that in a world that claims "all is fair in love." In a balanced relationship no one should lord over anyone else. Each person in the relationship should have equal time to shine.

Be a Girlfriend with Power

Do not sit around waiting for a boyfriend to fill your time. Get active in your interests and spend time with him around that. The more you develop yourself, the more interesting you are to others. I also asked the boys what is the biggest turn off in a girlfriend, and they said needy girls. They do not want the pressure of being everything to a girl. They said it was exhausting.

To be a girlfriend with power you have to understand love. The bible talks a lot about love. *"Love is patient, love is kind. It does not envy, it does not boast. It is not proud. It is not rude. It is not self-seeking, it is not easily angered, it keeps no records of wrongs. Love does not delight in evil but rejoices with the truth. It always protects, always trusts, always hopes, always perseveres"* (1 Corinthians 13:4-7).

Teenagers have a lot of emotion and lack experience to navigate it. Having an understanding of love will provide a basis. Love does not hurt you physically or emotionally. *"There is no fear in love. But perfect love drives out fear, because fear has to do with punishment. The one who fears is not made perfect in love"* (1 John 4:18). Love does not demand that you be someone other than who God created you to be. Love is not the act of sex. *"Flee from sexual immorality. All other sins a man commits are outside his body, but he who sins sexually sins against his own body".* (1 Corinthians 6:18)

Steps to being a girlfriend with power

Step one: Start with a full understanding that a relationship has two active members.

1. Make him call: No drop of a dime texted hook ups.
2. No last minute stuff: if he cannot plan ahead, too bad for him.
3. The second big turnoff is a bossy girlfriend. Give the poor guy some space.

Step two: Keep your own interests. Do not give up all your time with your friends or quit activities to be a girlfriend. A guy that expects you to give up all you are to merge into his life, his friends, be his 24/7 cheerleader is not showing you a caring nature. Also, a really quick way to lose a boyfriend is to give up all your interest to try to control him 24/7. You should be able to cheer him on Friday at his football game, and he should be able to cheer you on Saturday at your volleyball game. You should have no problem going shopping with your girls after school while he hangs with his boys. There has to be balance.

Step three: Never deny who you are. A very popular portrayal in the media is the girl who gives the starry eyed stare, with the giggle and perfect hair flip as a response to a guy of interest. And there is nothing wrong with that as long as it is not followed with a need to dumb yourself down. To discount your true value takes away what makes you interesting. Keeping up the act will quickly prove itself taxing. If all you have to offer is a sweet smile and awesome hair flip, you can imagine how dull it will get for him and for you.

The last step is most important. If it is not working for you move on. Teenagers have a short attention span, and your actions can be driven by a need for constant stimulation, constant movement mentally and physically. It is like keeping a fire burning. You have to feed the flame. The less care you give the fire, the lower the flame. The more care you give it, the bigger the flame. If you are in a relationship that is requiring a lot of you to keep it going, it is time to move on.

I picked the opening verse with care because it is such a great example of how being careless with your value, giving that value to whomever comes around will allow others to treat your value as carelessly as you gave it away. This is not limited to boys but also crosses into friendships as well. *"Do not give dogs what is sacred; do not throw your pearls to pigs if you do, they may trample them under their feet, and then turn and tear you to pieces. (Matthew 7:6)"*

Extra verses for you:

The body that is sown is perishable, it is raised imperishable; it is sown in dishonor, it is raised in glory; it is sown in weakness and raised in power; it is sown a natural body, it is raised a spiritual body.... (1 Corinthians 15:42-44).

You are God's Temple (1 Corinthians 3:16-17).

"God is love. Whoever lives in love lives in God, and God in him. In this way, love is made complete." (1 John 4:11-21) This is an important verse because how much you love yourself is how much you will allow others to love you.

11

```
┌─────────────────────────────────┐
│                                 │
- - - │          Bullying            │ - - -
│                                 │
└─────────────────────────────────┘
```

How we treat others is of serious concern to God and there are very strict words spoken about it. *"The tongue that brings healing is a tree of life, but a deceitful tongue crushes the spirit". (Proverbs 15:4)*

The Bible is filled with verses that discuss the dangers of the tongue. In this verse it says a deceitful tongue can crush the spirit. That is what bullying does, it crushes the spirit. The Bible warns *"Do not slander and speak against others; you are also speaking against God."* Just as you are created in God's image so is that classmate you are speaking deceitfully about. *"Do not judge, or you too will be judged. For the same way you judge others, you will be judged, and with the measure you use, it will be measured to you." (Matthew 7:1).* James chapter 3 is titled taming the tongue 3:9 says, *"With the tongue we praise our Lord and Father, and with it we curse men, who have been made in God's likeness". "Therefore, rid yourselves of all malice and deceit hypocrisy, envy, and slander of every kind". (1 Peter 2:1)* And there are plenty more warnings just like these.

An inner weakness cannot be substituted with physical strength.

Feeling threatened by someone else can be a driving force behind why we gossip, bully, virtually bully, and physically attack others. Bullying is not new, if you read the life of Jesus in your bible you will see they bullied Jesus also. We seek out others like us to make friends and make enemies of the rest.

Are you the bully or are you being bullied?

Media today glorifies bullying. Every tween show on the air portrays the "popular" girls as those who own the school, and to remain on top they must tear everyone else down around them. Being bullied today takes on many different forms; the computer and text medium have given people newfound courage while giving the ability to mass produce hurtful things and keep a level of anonymity. A coward's courage.

What steps should you take if you are being bullied?

I wish I could say to just ignore them, but that honestly does not do much. Kids are being bullied and for endless reasons never tell an adult. One reason is a fear that the adult will stand them in front of the class and say that everyone has to be nice to Priscilla, creating an even larger target on them. Bullying has gotten so much attention lately, unfortunately because of the number of kids who have hurt themselves or others. The schools are being forced to take steps to handle this problem. The old statement "kids will be kids" is no longer acceptable.

Some steps that can be taken

1. Find out what the schools policy on bullying is and hold the school accountable to follow it.

2. Facebook bullying - Save those messages to show authority figures involved in seeing you through this and shutdown your page.

3. Legal options - If the bullying becomes a legal matter, those text messages and Facebook things will be important.

4. If you feel that your situation is one that you can talk to your bully, do not give that bully an audience; the audience is where they gain their strength, so talk to them on your turf. Invite them over after school, or pull that person aside at school but do it one on one. Do not address the group.

Do not allow those bullies to make you feel alone and isolated. The number one deterrent to a bully is confidence. *"When they hurled their insults at him, he did not retaliate; when he suffered he made no threats. Instead, he entrusted himself to him who judges justly" (1 Peter 2:23).* When you know who you are and you are confident in that you can walk away. Does it still hurt? Yes, but instead of crushing your spirit it is a flesh wound that will heal. *"Do not be afraid of them; the Lord your God himself will fight for you" (Deuteronomy 3:22).* In other words, God's got your back.

The worst view to take in this position is the "eye for an eye" position that we tend to stand so strongly on. "She posted something bad about me on Facebook so I have to post something worse about her." This is a vicious cycle that will go around and around until someone loses big. It could be a crushed spirit or worse -- kids have lost their lives over it.

How they Bullied Jesus

They hated him. They vilified him. They betrayed him. They executed him.

They hated him. Jesus had many run-ins with his opposition. What drives hate? Fear, a fear that this person is better than me, a fear that I must knock others down to show how powerful I am. They have threatened my popularity... (*John 7:45-52*).

They betrayed him. *Then one of the twelve-the one called Judas Iscariot-went to the chief priest and asked, "What are you willing to give me if I hand him over to you?" So they counted out for him thirty silver coins. From then on Judas watched for an opportunity to hand him over (Matthew 26:14-16). Now the betrayer had arranged a signal with them: "The one I kiss is the man; arrest him." Going at once to Jesus, Judas said, "Greetings, Rabbi!" and kissed him. Jesus replied, "Friend, do what you came for." (Matthew 26:48-50).*

They vilified him. They vilified Jesus with gossip, insults, and untrue rumors. *But the chief priest and elders persuaded the crowd to ask for Barabbas and to have Jesus executed (Matthew 27:20) (full account Matthew 27:11-25).* This is one of many accounts of how they tried to vilify Jesus.

They executed Him. We do not hang innocent people on a cross today but we do mentally execute people, and some we even physically assault. Recall that the "girl fight" has become so popular that it is on YouTube, songs are written about it, and it is in movies. This girl fight is often a group of girls that attack one girl. Sound familiar? *A group of people beat him taunted, and insulted him, hung him on the cross to die (Matthew 27:32-56).* They did it to Jesus.

But guess what?
He rose from that cross. If you are the person being bullied this is a real message: *"If the world hates you just keep in mind that it hated me first" (John 15:18).* You have been given the ability to rise above those people who come against you. Jesus never gave in to their attacks, and he never denied who he was. He lived a great life as an example to each of us how to get through.

If you are the bully.
This is a personality trait that requires strength to change. You must take the time and find scripture on how God deals with bullies. Understand that using strength to gain what seems like popularity will show its true self in the zero hour, when you are in need of a true friend and you realize how alone and empty your life really is. How many people are actually using you for that strength to forge their way? Once that has happened they will abandon you in the same fashion that you have abandoned others in your path. You possess no cross big enough to keep a child of God down. You may cause a slight delay, but you cannot keep them down. And when they rise their light will shine so brightly it will put you to shame. Very harsh words, but the Bible's are even sharper.

12

Salvation

'If you confess with your mouth, "Jesus is Lord," and believe in your heart that God raised him from the dead, you will be saved. For it is with your heart that you believe and are justified, and it is with your mouth that you confess and are saved. (Romans 10:9-10)

Salvation is the foundation of our beliefs as Christians. That God gave his son to die on the cross for me, to deliver me from my sin and open the door for a direct relationship with Him.

What did I gain from the Cross?

Jesus' death and resurrection on the cross goes much further than Forgiveness of sin. Do not misunderstand and think that is not enough, because that alone is a gift with value far beyond our understanding, but it does not stop there. The cross can be limited to what it means to our future in heaven. The missing piece is that the cross also gives us a life right now, here on this earth: a life in relationship with God that brings strength, a covering, victory, and love. Some Christians spend their entire walk with God focused on "when I get to heaven..." *But God said "I have come that they may have life and have it to the full." (John 10:10)*

The Cross gives you a relationship with God

Throughout our lives we will need different things from God. We may need God the Father. *"You are all sons of God through faith in Christ Jesus" (Galatians 3:26),* God the friend. *"Greater love has no one than this that he lay down his life for his friends. You are my friends if you do what I command" (John 15:13-14).* God as your teacher and guide. *"I will ask the Father, and he will give you another Counselor to be with you forever" (John 14:15, 15:26,16:7,16:12-15* just to name a few) God as light *"I am the light of the world. Whoever follows me will never walk in darkness, but will have the light of life." (John 8:12).*

Never put God in a box, limiting him to a distant land called heaven. He is here for you now in the way you need Him. I have just put together a small view of God, but trust me when I say, when you allow Him into your everyday lives He will show you the limitless ways He is available to you.

The cross gives you strength

This is not a strength based on muscles or power but strength that gives you courage. Following God seems so simple: say a prayer, try to be good, and *boom* a golden ticket to heaven. There is someone else after your soul; there is a devil working to make sure you never live up to your potential. You may go to heaven but Satan will make sure you are miserable while you take the journey.

How do you fight against this devil? You don't. WHAT? You go through God. In Luke chapter 4, Jesus was tempted by the devil and he did not argue with the devil or fight against him. Instead each of his responses started with *"It is written."* He spoke the word of God. You do not even have to come up with witty comebacks -- there is such power in the word of God, you just have to speak it directly to the devil. The next time the devil plants the idea in your mind such as "I'm not good enough," you do not accept that. You instantly say "according to my God it is Good".

"In the beginning was the Word and the Word was with God, and the Word was God. He was with God In the beginning" *(John 1:1-2). I have given you authority to trample on snakes and scorpions and to overcome all the power of the enemy: nothing will harm you (Luke 10:19).*

The cross gives you victory

Victory over what? Satan; you do not have to spend your life fighting Satan. The last verse says that God already gave you authority. The trick is to take your focus off the temptations of Satan and put it on the victory you have already been given from God. *"We know that anyone born of God does not continue to sin; the one who was born of God keeps him safe, and the evil one cannot harm him"(1 John 5:18).*

You also have victory over the challenges of life, the day to day. *"For everyone born of God overcomes the world. This is the victory that has overcome the world, even our faith. Who is it that overcomes the world? Only he who believes that Jesus is the Son of God (1 John 5:4-5).*

My Story:

I feel I need to share my story because people have many ideas of what the moment will be like when they ask God into their lives. Some expect the heavens to open, the earth to shake, and God will wave a magic wand and change their lives forever. We are talking about God and anything is possible, but for me it did not go down quite like that.

As I mentioned earlier, I was raised in the church. I do not even remember the exact day I asked God into my life. I have met many people who can tell you in detail about their experience. I have heard of people being overcome with emotion, some have been overtaken by the Holy Spirit and dropped to the floor, and some people even started speaking in tongues. Not so exciting for me.

I have always felt God in my life, so for me the moment of change came when I stepped out of my parents' Christian shadow and stood on my own two spiritual legs. I got an overwhelming awareness.

What does that mean? God started to lead me in my life. I did not make many changes in my life when this took place, but now everyday things would actually bother me. When I faced the consequences of my actions I felt God ask me if it was worth it. When I made bad choices (which I did a lot), after the dust settled God would show me how He was protecting me.

I was very popular in high school and college. I got pregnant when I was twenty years old; as my friends were turning twenty-one and partying I was playing house. My friends and I went in different directions, and I had to deal with a LOT of loneliness. I went from having friends all around me, the life of the party, to no friends at all, none, not a one. This struggle lasted a long time but through it all, God made His presence known to me in the way I needed it.

I grew with God in this time instead of sulking about not having any friends. I grew a friendship with God. My attitude changed about friendship and life. I am a different person all together.

So remember when you pray, God will give you what you need in the way you need it. Do not look over the fence to compare your experience with your neighbors'. There will only be two outcomes from that: Disappointment (you are doing things better than me) or Pride (I am doing better than you).

Once you ask God into your life the moment can be so exciting, but when the morning comes and you make a mistake the first thought Satan can put into your head is that you have already lost your salvation. It is only day one and you are already out. Salvation is a journey, a journey you will take with God. Recognize what you have done, and ask God to forgive you and enjoy your journey. You cannot lose God. You can turn away from Him but He will never leave you from this moment on.

My Prayer for salvation:

Father I need you, I am a sinner Lord and I need forgiveness from you. I thank you Lord for giving your son Jesus for me so that I can have a relationship with you. Help me to grow in you Lord, fill me with your Spirit so I can be a better daughter, sister, friend, and leader for your kingdom. Use your Spirit to guide my steps Father, put your teachers and guides in my path, and use me Lord for your will. Not my will Lord but your will be done. In Jesus name, amen.

Jesus Prays for all believers *(John 17:20-25)*

"My prayer is not for them alone. I pray also for those who will believe in me through their message, that all of them may be one, Father, just as you are in me and I am in you. May they also be in us so that the world may believe that you have sent me. I have given them the glory that you gave me, that they may be one as we are one: I in them and you in me. May they be brought to complete unity to let the world know that you sent me and have loved them even as you have loved me. Father, I want those you have given me to be with me where I am, and to see my glory, the glory you have given me because you loved me before the creation of the world. Righteous Father, though the world does not know you, I know you, and they know that you have sent me. I have made you known to them, and will continue to make you known in order that the love you have for me may be in them and that I myself may be in them."

*In Him and through faith in him we may approach
God with freedom and confidence. Ephesians 3:12*

*Then they asked him, "What must we do to do the work
God requires?" Jesus answered, "The work of God is
this: to believe in the one he has sent." John 6:28-29*

All scriptures were taken from the New International Version
(NIV) of the bible.

Webster's American dictionary was also used throughout
this book.

Journal

O *Lord, you have searched me and you know me. You know*
when I sit and when I rise; you perceive my thoughts from
afar. You discern my going out and my lying down; you are
familiar with all my ways. Before a word is on my tongue you
know it completely, O Lord. You hem me in-behind and before;
you have laid your hand upon me. Such knowledge is too
wonderful for me, too lofty for me to attain. Where can I go from
your Spirit? Where can I flee from your presence? If I go up to the
heavens, you are there; if I make my bed in the depths, you are
there. If I rise on the wings of the dawn, if I settle on the far side of
the sea, even there your hand will guide me, your right hand will
hold me fast. If I say, "Surely the darkness will hide me and the
light become night around me," even the darkness will not be dark
to you; the night will shine like the day, for darkness is as light
to you. For you created my inmost being; you knit me together
in my mother's womb. I praise you because I am fearfully and
wonderfully made; your works are wonderful, I know that full
well. My frame was not hidden from you when I was made in
the secret place. When I was woven together in the depths of the
earth, your eyes saw my unformed body. All the days ordained
for me were written in your book before one of them came to be.
How precious to me are your thoughts, O God! How vast is the
sum of them! Were I to count them they would outnumber the
grains of sand. When I awake, I am still with you.

(Psalms 139:1-18)